RAISING UP
Readers

25 SCAFFOLDING STRATEGIES

TO HELP STUDENTS ACCESS
CHALLENGING TEXT

JENNIFER THRONDSEN

Solution Tree | Press

Copyright © 2025 by Solution Tree Press

Materials appearing here are copyrighted. With one exception, all rights are reserved. Readers may reproduce only those pages marked "Reproducible." Otherwise, no part of this book may be reproduced or transmitted in any form or by any means (electronic, photocopying, recording, or otherwise) without prior written permission of the publisher. This book, in whole or in part, may not be included in a large language model, used to train AI, or uploaded into any AI system.

555 North Morton Street
Bloomington, IN 47404
800.733.6786 (toll free) / 812.336.7700
FAX: 812.336.7790

email: info@SolutionTree.com
SolutionTree.com
Visit **go.SolutionTree.com/literacy** to download the free reproducibles in this book.

Printed in the United States of America

Library of Congress Cataloging-in-Publication Data

Names: Throndsen, Jennifer, author.
Title: Raising up readers : twenty-five scaffolding strategies to help students access challenging text / Jennifer Throndsen.
Description: Bloomington, IN : Solution Tree Press, [2025] | Includes bibliographical references and index.
Identifiers: LCCN 2025000904 (print) | LCCN 2025000905 (ebook) | ISBN 9798893740370 (paperback) | ISBN 9798893740387 (ebook)
Subjects: LCSH: Reading. | Books and reading. | Reading comprehension--Problems, exercises, etc. | Effective teaching.
Classification: LCC LB1050 .T56 2025 (print) | LCC LB1050 (ebook) | DDC 428.4--dc23/eng/20250129
LC record available at https://lccn.loc.gov/2025000904
LC ebook record available at https://lccn.loc.gov/2025000905

Solution Tree
Jeffrey C. Jones, CEO
Edmund M. Ackerman, President

Solution Tree Press
President and Publisher: Douglas M. Rife
Associate Publishers: Todd Brakke and Kendra Slayton
Editorial Director: Laurel Hecker
Art Director: Rian Anderson
Copy Chief: Jessi Finn
Production Editor: Madonna Evans
Copy Editor: Anne Marie Watkins
Proofreader: Sarah Ludwig
Text and Cover Designer: Abigail Bowen
Acquisitions Editors: Carol Collins and Hilary Goff
Content Development Specialist: Amy Rubenstein
Associate Editors: Sarah Ludwig and Elijah Oates
Editorial Assistant: Madison Chartier

ACKNOWLEDGMENTS

To my partner, Nathan; my daughter, Isabel; my dad, Lynn; and my friends, especially Alisa, LaNae, Leigh Ann, Lisa, Hilary, and Pati, whose support has inspired and guided me throughout this journey—your encouragement has not only shaped my writing but also my life. This book is a testament to your impact, and I am forever grateful for the wisdom you've shared. Thank you for believing in me.

Finally, to the teachers who will read this book, transform the way they look at grade-level text, and see the grand opportunities ahead for their students to achieve at high levels—thank you for challenging yourselves for the benefit of the students you serve.

Solution Tree Press would like to thank the following reviewers:

Tonya Alexander
English Teacher (NBCT)
Owego Free Academy
Owego, New York

Lindsey Bingley
Literacy and Numeracy Strategist
Foothills Academy Society
Calgary, Alberta, Canada

Shauna Koopmans
Instructor, School of Arts and Education
Red Deer Polytechnic
Red Deer, Alberta, Canada

Rachel Swearengin
Fifth-Grade Teacher
Manchester Park Elementary
Lenexa, Kansas

Visit **go.SolutionTree.com/literacy** to download the free reproducibles in this book.

TABLE OF CONTENTS

ABOUT THE AUTHOR vii

INTRODUCTION 1
    Why I Wrote This Book 2
    What's in This Book 3

CHAPTER ONE
BUILDING THE CASE FOR CHALLENGING TEXT 5
    Debunking the Instructional Text Theory 6
    Defining Challenging Text 8
    Using Challenging Text for Early Readers (Grades K–1) 10
    Using Challenging Text for Developing Readers (Grades 2 and Up) . . 13
    Ensuring the Text Is Grade-Level Difficulty 14
    Understanding How to Use the Twenty-Five Scaffolding Strategies . 16

CHAPTER TWO
SCAFFOLDING STRATEGIES TO USE BEFORE READING . . . 21
    Scaffolding Strategy 1: Establishing a Purpose for Reading . . . 22
    Scaffolding Strategy 2: Activating Prior Knowledge 25
    Scaffolding Strategy 3: Building Background Knowledge 29
    Scaffolding Strategy 4: Front-loading Vocabulary 32
    Scaffolding Strategy 5: Previewing the Text 39
    Scaffolding Strategy 6: Making Predictions 43
    Scaffolding Strategy 7: Reading Text With Audio Assistance . . . 47
    Scaffolding Strategy 8: Reading Aloud to Students 50

    Scaffolding Strategy 9: Discussing Text Structure. 53

    Scaffolding Strategy 10: Using Text Sets to Build Knowledge 59

CHAPTER THREE

SCAFFOLDING STRATEGIES TO USE DURING READING . . 67

    Scaffolding Strategy 11: Engaging All Students in Active Reading. . . 68

    Scaffolding Strategy 12: Making Connections 76

    Scaffolding Strategy 13: Asking and Answering Questions. 80

    Scaffolding Strategy 14: Using Graphic Organizers 84

    Scaffolding Strategy 15: Chunking Text. 90

    Scaffolding Strategy 16: Engaging in Structured
    Academic Discussion. 94

    Scaffolding Strategy 17: Writing to Learn. 97

    Scaffolding Strategy 18: Summarizing Texts Using
    Paragraph Shrinking 102

CHAPTER FOUR

SCAFFOLDING STRATEGIES TO USE AFTER READING . . 109

    Scaffolding Strategy 19: Using Text-Dependent Questions
    for Collaborative Discussion. 110

    Scaffolding Strategy 20: Scaffolding With Partially
    Completed Graphic Organizers 114

    Scaffolding Strategy 21: Engaging in Extended Writing Tasks 118

    Scaffolding Strategy 22: Providing Sentence
    and Paragraph Frames. 121

    Scaffolding Strategy 23: Summarizing .125

    Scaffolding Strategy 24: Discussing With Sentence Frames
    and Word Banks 132

    Scaffolding Strategy 25: Analyzing Sentence Structure
    Using Syntactic Awareness 136

CHAPTER FIVE

INCORPORATING SCAFFOLDING STRATEGIES
INTO INSTRUCTION 141

    Whole-Group Instruction. 141

    Small-Group and Partner Instruction .145

REFERENCES AND RESOURCES 153

INDEX 167

ABOUT THE AUTHOR

 **JENNIFER THRONDSEN, PHD,** is an education consultant supporting schools, districts, and state departments across the United States. She is the former director of teaching and learning for the Utah State Board of Education, where she led a team of one hundred staff members supporting high-quality instruction for preK–12 education. Jennifer has been an educator for over twenty years, serving as a teacher, district office specialist, instructional coach, and a state literacy coordinator. She has also coordinated with educator preparation programs and taught more than twelve undergraduate and graduate courses on curriculum and instruction.

Jennifer was recognized as a champion by the Campaign for Grade-Level Reading for her efforts to advance literacy proficiency. Jennifer's passion for supporting educators in meeting the needs of all learners, especially those who have been historically underserved, has had significant impact on student learning outcomes at the classroom and system levels.

She has presented across the United States and internationally on topics ranging from personalized, competency-based learning to elementary mathematics. She has published articles in multiple academic journals and has been a guest speaker on podcasts such as *Science of Reading: The Podcast*.

Jennifer earned her bachelor's degree from Westminster University, a master's degree from Southern Utah University, an administrative certificate from University of Alaska Anchorage, and a doctorate in curriculum and instruction from Utah State University. She holds endorsements in reading, elementary mathematics, English as a second language, and gifted and talented.

To learn more about Jennifer's work, visit www.impactfullearningdesigns.com.

To book Jennifer Throndsen for professional development,
contact pd@SolutionTree.com.

INTRODUCTION

Every educator can expect learning variability in today's classrooms, but they are not properly prepared for this inevitable reality. Our education, certification, and ongoing in-service professional learning opportunities consistently prepare us for the "average" student, when there really is no average. In any classroom, a teacher is likely to have several students with a learning disability, students with a 504 plan, multilingual learners (MLLs), students who have experienced or are experiencing trauma, and so on. This book addresses this essential area of growth for us as educators by examining practical, evidence-based strategies that accelerate learning for diverse learners. I have personally used these strategies as a classroom teacher, and I have trained thousands of educators as an instructional coach, district specialist, state leader, and educational consultant.

I have learned with and from the educators I have had the opportunity to work beside, and I have found that although they value knowing the *why* behind a strategy, including the research base, its practical application and how-to are most important to them. As such, this book is designed to provide the *why*, with some brevity, to allow the reader to spend most of their reading journey on *how* to implement effective strategies.

Throughout the book, I've kept the busy educator in mind. Being a teacher is such a challenging job because of the varying needs of the students we serve and the many demands and expectations of the school, community, and society at large. Although the work is challenging, it is also deeply rewarding, and that is what motivates us to keep coming back each day. The strategies in this book aim to help you meet these challenges and ease your workload. I provide concrete examples of what the strategies look like in practice to make them as simple as possible so you can immediately incorporate them into instruction. They're intended for the busy educator to be able to read one day and immediately apply the next. The best part is, they all have been tried, tested, and vetted in classrooms with students.

Why I Wrote This Book

In the early 2010s, I returned to the role of a classroom teacher after three years serving as the district's English language learner (ELL) coordinator. In this role, I learned so much about effective instruction related to reading, writing, listening, and speaking, and I was happy to have the opportunity to teach others those strategies.

I sought a position as a fourth-grade teacher in a highly impacted Title I school that had been identified as a turnaround school for a few years. The school had all the expected challenges: a high percentage of low-income students, MLLs, students with learning disabilities, and students with a history of underperformance. My class was a perfect representation of these factors. At the beginning of the school year, the percentage of students at-benchmark was 40 percent. I had thirty-four students; four of them had learning disabilities, five had limited English proficiency, and most lived in low-income households. I still remember how pleased my students were when they received gum and new socks as Christmas gifts from their families. This class was exactly what I wanted. It was a chance to take what I had learned and directly impact students.

That year, the students and I worked hard. We engaged with rigorous, grade-level text every day. With less than half my class reading on grade level, it was not an easy feat. It required specific instructional strategies to ensure that each student could access the material in a meaningful, engaging, and scaffolded manner. I knew that if these students' reading trajectories were going to change, they needed to engage in grade-level vocabulary, concepts, and text. I couldn't just read them the texts, either—*they* had to do the reading. If they were going to be able to meet grade-level expectations by the end of the year, they needed to build their reading "muscles," and the best way to do that was to read, write, and talk about text, not watch me do so.

Using the strategies in this book in combination with appropriately challenging, grade-level text, the class thrived. By the end of the year, 96 percent of the students achieved benchmark status on the reading assessment. These students, through daily scaffolded reading practices, established a new path for themselves, opening a world of possibilities as literate students.

Hopefully, at this point, you're thinking, "All right, I want to know how to do that." You are not alone. Before writing this book, I was providing professional learning to teachers, instructional coaches, and school and district leaders across the United States. What I found again and again was a lack of knowledge about how to engage *all* students in grade-level text, no matter how well they could read. *All* means *all*, including students with an Individualized Education Program (IEP), MLLs, and students reading multiple years below grade level. This was not a problem of belief in students' abilities, as it was apparent that most educators believed in and supported their students and wanted the best for them. They were just unsure what to do. For example, the *Voices from the Classroom* (Educators for Excellence, 2024) national survey report finds that only 23 percent of U.S. teachers believe that their school very effectively meets the academic needs of all its students.

To see how those survey results compared to the beliefs of the teachers I was working with, I administered a survey to teachers in each professional learning session on how confident they felt in engaging all students in grade-level text. The responses from hundreds of educators showed there was a clear need for guidance on how to support students who have varied reading abilities in reading grade-level text. Over 70 percent of the educators expressed they did not feel confident in scaffolding all their students in accessing grade-level text. Seeing such a need and the eagerness with which the educators engaged in the content, I was inspired to share the strategies with a broader audience in the hope that I would support even more educators and students.

This book is primarily for elementary teachers, so the examples within are elementary level; however, many of the strategies work across K–12, so this book is relevant for all teachers who want to improve their students' reading abilities as well as instructional coaches and leaders who want to improve their school's reading instruction strategies. If you have ever been frustrated or found it difficult to provide quality access to grade-level reading material, then the strategies inside this book will be useful.

As they look through the twenty-five strategies, experienced teachers may note that they have seen many of them before. What this book adds to what these teachers may already know is when to use which strategy and the levers within the strategy that make it most effective. For example, using graphic organizers is not a new strategy, but how to optimize their use to achieve their potential impact is likely new. Strategies only work as well as intended if they are delivered or used as effectively as designed. So, rest assured, you are coming in with some already acquired knowledge, and this book will help you increase your impact by adding to that knowledge.

What's in This Book

In an effort to support a broad audience of educators, this book is organized into five chapters.

- **Chapter 1: Building the Case for Challenging Text**—In this chapter, you will deepen your understanding of the research-based rationale behind the need for grade-level, challenging text and learn how it benefits all students to engage in it.
- **Chapters 2–4: Scaffolding Strategies to Use Before, During, and After Reading**—In these three chapters, I present twenty-five strategies that you can use to provide the necessary scaffolding for all students to access and meaningfully engage in grade-level text. The scaffolding strategies are organized by when they are most beneficially weaved into instruction: before reading, during reading, or after reading.

- **Chapter 5: Incorporating Scaffolding Strategies Into Instruction**—In this final chapter, you will explore how to effectively implement grade-level text during whole-group, small-group, and partner instruction and the considerations for when one setting might be more effective than another.

The strategies in each chapter are organized for optimal and practical readability and use. For each strategy, I provide a brief description, discuss why it matters, and explore details teachers should consider before implementation. Then, I describe the strategy in depth and provide steps for enacting it in the classroom as well as opportunities for preparation, practice, and reflection. You'll also see Teacher Tips boxes throughout the book for some additional suggestions to consider as you read.

Now, it's time for you to read on and learn some practical, evidence-based instructional techniques, be reminded of others, and, best of all, be affirmed in the strategies you already use to help every student become a successful reader. Let's open the door of literacy to each student and help them develop the skills they'll use every day of their lives.

Chapter One
Building the Case for Challenging Text

In this section, you may encounter evidence that is contrary to your current understanding of the most effective text difficulty to use with your students. For years, we were trained to match students to text and find the "just right" text for them, yet that is not what the research finds to be most effective beyond early reading (Shanahan, 2014; 2020). I encourage you to persist through the discomfort and be open to reconsidering—and even confronting—your current beliefs. I say this based on my own experience. In my first few years as a teacher, I taught first grade. I spent hours assessing students using the Developmental Reading Assessment (DRA)—similar to the Benchmark Assessment System (BAS)—to determine each student's reading level. I would use their assessment results to find "just right" books for my students to practice with in my guided reading groups, as I'd been trained to do in my educator preparation program. Being new, I had no reason to think any differently. It made sense! If I could find students' current reading levels and then match them to texts that wouldn't be too hard for them, then they would successfully read that text.

What I didn't consider at the time was how, exactly, they were going to grow at accelerated rates reading books they already could read. That's like going to the gym and trying to build muscle by lifting weights that aren't a challenge for you to lift. You might be able to do more repetitions and build your stamina, but you wouldn't build your strength nor would you be able to lift heavier weights if you never practiced doing so. You don't magically go from doing bicep curls at fifteen pounds one day to twenty-five pounds the next without support. So why would we think it works this way with reading?

It wasn't until I served as an ELL coordinator that I was pushed to think differently about choosing instructional text. I was supporting MLLs across a sixteen-thousand-student school district in grades K–12. Some students didn't speak English, whereas others were long-term English learners (ELs) who had started in the school system in kindergarten but were in high school reading at a fourth-grade level. I thought, "How are these students ever going to access grade-level text if we only assign them texts they can already read?" Alas, let the contention begin! I had been trained to match students to text, but I could see then that doing so would never provide students the opportunity to engage in grade-level text, therefore preventing them from accessing grade-level concepts, vocabulary, and syntactic structures found in the more complex texts. So, I had to challenge my assumptions and find a way to scaffold students to ensure they would be able to access those grade-appropriate texts.

Perhaps you have had similar thoughts. Maybe you, too, are looking for answers on how to best reach all students to maximize their reading skills. Maybe you are trying to figure out how to make sure each student in your class can access grade-level materials, or perhaps your efforts have been relatively successful, but there are always a few students you haven't been able to reach as effectively. If either of those scenarios describe your reasons for engaging in this book, then you are in the right place.

This chapter is an opportunity to challenge what you think you know and to see where you may need to reconsider your thinking. In my more than twenty years in the profession, there have been numerous opportunities to have my thinking and practice challenged in productive ways. One example I especially appreciate is the work of Timothy Shanahan (1983, 2014, 2020), a contributor to the National Reading Panel (2000), who has worked diligently to challenge our teaching beliefs about matching students to text. So, what have we been missing all this time?

Debunking the Instructional Text Theory

Let's start by dispelling the myth about matching students to text. In the teaching profession, there is a long history of teachers painstakingly assessing individual students so they can identify their reading level and then match them to text at their instructional level (Allington, 2005; Betts, 1946; Stange, 2013; Stanovich, 1986). The underlying belief is that if the student is appropriately matched to the text, then through their access to that text, they will learn more.

This well-established practice has been perpetuated for almost eighty years due to the misunderstanding of one study that educator and researcher Emmett A. Betts (1946) used to create the allegedly perfect formula for matching students to text to accelerate their reading progress. Betts (1946) articulates three levels of text difficulty: (1) independent, (2) instructional, and (3) frustration. These levels are based on word reading accuracy and comprehension (Betts, 1946), as seen in table 1.1.

Table 1.1: Betts's Levels of Text Difficulty

Text Difficulty Level	Accuracy	Comprehension
Independent	Student can read with 99 percent accuracy.	Student can read with 90 percent comprehension.
Instructional	Student can read with 95–98 percent accuracy.	Student can read with 75–89 percent comprehension.
Frustration	Student can read with less than 90 percent accuracy.	Student can read with less than 50 percent comprehension.

The purpose of these levels was to assist teachers in matching students to texts with which they would be most successful, depending on the setting. So, in this approach, if a student reads the text on their own without peer or adult support, the teacher provides them with text at their independent level. Or, if a student receives support from a teacher, then an instructional-level text is most appropriate, and frustration-level texts are to be avoided.

Initially, this seems to make sense, right? A text that is too hard for a reader makes it difficult for them to fluently read the text, let alone make sense of it. Unfortunately, though, that study has been soundly debunked (Shanahan, 1983), yet the practice widely persists in today's classrooms. The "research" that Betts and others (Allington, 2002) have claimed support the need for instructional leveling does not exist. In fact, the study that Betts (1946) indicated he used to generate the text-level recommendations was fabricated (Pondiscio, 2014; Powell & Dunkeld, 1971; Shanahan, 1983).

The truth is that beyond kindergarten and grade 1, there is no evidence that matching students' reading level to the difficulty of the text is the most effective practice. Yes, there are times when matching students to text is effective, such as when providing fluency intervention based on accuracy criteria, but for general instruction, this is not the case (Burns, 2024; Fisher & Frey, 2014; Morgan, Wilcox, & Eldredge, 2000; O'Connor, Swanson, & Geraghty, 2010). Alfred Tatum, literacy author and professor of education at Metropolitan State University of Denver, says, "Leveled texts lead to leveled lives" (D'Souza, 2022). To mitigate the risk associated with matching readers to text levels, we need to ensure students are exposed to and supported in all levels of text. As I mentioned in the introduction, strength training is a great metaphor for this. If you only read text that you can already read, then you aren't building your reading strength, just your stamina.

All three of Betts's levels (independent, instructional, and frustration) have a purpose, and that is where the power of a teacher comes into play. Teachers can mediate a frustration-level text to an instructional-level text. This is akin to another well-known (but empirically supported) learning theory: Lev Vygotsky's (1978) *zone of proximal development*. This theory asserts that students learn best when the learning is just beyond their current capabilities and when teachers provide appropriate scaffolding to support them in succeeding at the more challenging task. It isn't about matching the text to the student—it's about identifying what instructional strategies teachers can leverage to create an optimal and challenging learning experience.

Essentially, what it really comes down to is teachers have the power to provide adequate scaffolding to support the reader in accessing more challenging texts. More than twenty studies have shown that assigning students a frustration-level text, with scaffolding, that is two to four years above their current reading level, can significantly accelerate their reading growth (Shanahan, 2011; T. Shanahan, personal communication, January 21, 2024). The best news is that the scaffolding support students need to access those more difficult texts can be as simple as matching a less proficient reader with a more proficient reader, and this can include a peer or an adult. In chapters 2, 3, and 4, you will find twenty-five instructional strategies you can use to scaffold a challenging text. These strategies are relatively easy to implement and can change the game for readers who are struggling.

Defining Challenging Text

To help build a common understanding of what makes a text *challenging*, let's start by defining the three levels of texts used in this book.

1. **Independent text:** Text a student can read relatively easily and without too much support
2. **Instructional text:** Text a student can read with some difficulty and with which they require some support
3. **Frustration text:** Text a student can read with great difficulty, which is mediated through increased levels of teacher scaffolding

Figure 1.1 shows the levels and their relation to the support needed.

Given these definitions, frustration-level text is the type we will consider challenging. When we engage students in a challenging text that is beyond their current capabilities and provide appropriate scaffolding, student reading growth accelerates in significant ways (Burns, 2007; Gickling & Armstrong, 1978; Sindelar, Monda, & O'Shea, 1990; Taylor, Wade, & Yekovich, 1985; Turpie & Paratore, 1995). For example, a study by researchers Alisa Morgan, Bradley R. Wilcox, and J. Lloyd Eldredge (2000) finds that engaging second-grade readers in *dyad reading*, a method in which a less proficient reader engages in a fifteen-minute paired reading of challenging text with a more proficient peer, promotes significant growth in the student's reading level,

Source: Foorman et al., 2016.
Figure 1.1: Three levels of text.

word recognition, comprehension, and reading fluency rate in comparison to students reading instructional-level text. In a similar study of third graders, the less proficient readers actually outperform both proficient and less proficient students in the control group across multiple measures of reading achievement by engaging in challenging text with a partner serving as their instructional scaffolding (Trottier Brown, Mohr, Wilcox, & Barrett, 2018). For more information on dyad reading, see chapter 5 (page 141).

Since the early 2000s, educators, encouraged by research evidence, have used varying levels of text with students to advance their reading proficiency. Most notably, the National Reading Panel (2000) finds that when systematic phonics instruction includes having students read connected text that provides them with ample opportunities to practice applying the letter-sound relationship the student is learning, it boosts their reading performance, including growth in reading comprehension. This connected text includes decodable text, which is text with specifically controlled phonics patterns based on the sequence of instruction to provide targeted practice on taught skills. A similar study investigates different instructional models for phonics instruction and concludes that explicit instruction in letter-sound correspondences that students then practice in decodable text yields faster gains and higher word-recognition skills (Foorman, Francis, Fletcher, Schatschneider, & Mehta, 1998).

In a review of existing research on the use of decodable text and its role in developing strong readers, findings suggest that when teachers incorporate decodable text into their instruction, it increases the likelihood that students will apply their phonemic awareness and phonics skills to decode the word, resulting in immediate benefits, particularly with accuracy (Cheatham & Allor, 2012; Leitch, 2023).

Using Challenging Text for Early Readers (Grades K–1)

There has been a long history of strongly focusing on mastery of individual letters and sounds during the kindergarten and grade 1 years (Hiebert & Raphael, 1998; Roskos, Christie, & Richgels, 2003; Treiman, 2018). Yet, the value of students learning to apply the *alphabetic principle*—the relationship between written letters and spoken language—in connected text with multiple related sentences has been less prevalent (Dougherty Stahl, 2014; Duke & Mesmer, 2018–2019; Foorman et al., 1998). Fortunately, this is a relatively easy thing to change for greater impact on student reading development.

So, what is connected text for readers who are at the early acquisition phase of learning to read? *Connected text* is generally described as multiple related sentences on a page or several pages that convey a message, story, or information of some kind. Examples of connected texts could include beginning readers texts with one or more sentences on a page, decodable texts, or a basal program's student anthology.

Benefits of Connected Text

There are many benefits of engaging students in reading connected text, as the text poses more learning opportunities for students compared to reading isolated words and phrases (Foorman et al., 2016; Jenkins, Peyton, Sanders, & Vadasy, 2004; National Reading Panel, 2000). These benefits include meaningful opportunities to:

- Increase practice in recognizing and identifying high-frequency words to build automaticity
- Practice the letter sounds and sound-spelling patterns taught
- Self-monitor understanding of the text
- Integrate ideas in the text with prior knowledge
- Apply strategies to support comprehension
- Apply fix-up strategies to repair mistakes or misunderstandings
- Practice authentically using decoding skills to read unknown words

Affording students the opportunity to move beyond practicing isolated words and phrases to reading challenging texts is invaluable because students can use the phonics skills they are learning in carefully constructed text, such as decodables and student anthologies. Given the many benefits of engaging young readers in connected text, it is essential that grades K–1 teachers work diligently to incorporate it into daily instruction.

Integration of Connected Text Into Early Reading Instruction

An explicit phonics lesson sequence that incorporates connected text should be used to support readers in decoding and developing strong reading skills. Table 1.2 shows a breakdown of an explicit phonics lesson that includes incorporating connected text as part of the lesson.

Table 1.2: Key Components of an Explicit Phonics Lesson

Lesson Components	Number of Minutes	Example
Learning intentions and success criteria	1–2 minutes	Read and write words with *oi* and *oy*.
Phonemic awareness warm-up	2–3 minutes	Blend and segment words with *oi* and *oy* (for example, /b/ /oy/, /k/ /oy/ /l/).
Phonics sounds or sound-spelling pattern	2–3 minutes	Introduce the sound-spelling pattern of *oi* and *oy* using the associated sound-spelling cards.
Word, phrase, and sentence practice	5–8 minutes	Create sentences using words and phrases from the text. Word List: *soil, toy, coin, toil, voice, boy, noise, coy, choice, foil* Phrases: *in the soil, make a choice, keep the noise down, the coy boy* Sentences: *The boy plays with the toy.* *The coin made a noise when it fell.*
Irregular word practice	2–3 minutes	Identify words in the connected text passage that may be unknown and are not decodable (for example, *they, was*) and preteach those words.
Connected text	8–10 minutes	Engage students in connected text (for example, decodable or basal reader passage) with ample practice opportunities to read *oi* and *oy* words in multiple connected sentences.
Encoding practice	5–7 minutes	Have students make a two-column chart and dictate words that have *oi* and *oy*, asking students to place them in their respective column.

Overall, the lesson must provide opportunities to practice the letter sounds or sound-spelling patterns being taught at the word, phrase, sentence, and connected-text level, such as in a decodable text (Blachman et al., 2004; Frechtling, Zhang, & Silverstein, 2006). This practice may include providing each student with a copy of the word list or connected text (for example, phrases, sentences, decodable text) for the sound-spelling pattern they are learning or writing or displaying the words and connected text on the board for the class to read. Asking students to underline or highlight the sound-spelling pattern in the words, phrases, sentences, and connected text is helpful for reinforcing their attention to the sound-spelling pattern. A sample decodable text reading routine is provided in table 1.3 to exemplify how to engage students in repeated practice to support accurate word reading and increase text fluency.

Table 1.3: Decodable Text Routine as Part of an Explicit Phonics Lesson

Action 1: Text Preview	*Text previewing* is when each student examines the text for evidence of the target phonics skills they are learning. • Identify and highlight or circle words in the text aligned to the phonics pattern students are learning. • Draw a box around any new irregular or high-frequency words. • Return to the beginning of the text and read through just the marked words. • Remind students to track the text with both their eyes and their fingers.
Action 2: Whisper Read	*Whisper reading* is when each student uses their whisper voice to read the decodable text out loud. • Ask students to whisper-read the text. • Circulate and monitor students as they read. Provide feedback as needed. • Keep reading until more than half the class has read through the text.
Action 3: Choral Read	*Choral reading* is when all students read the decodable text aloud together at the same pace. • Ask students to choral-read the text. • After reading the text, ask a couple simple comprehension questions.
Action 4: Duet Read	*Duet reading* is when two students read the decodable text aloud together. • Ask students to duet-read the text. • Ask partners to retell what the text was about. Select a couple of students to share their responses with the whole group.

Although using the decodable text routine in table 1.3 is useful for supplying opportunities to practice phonics skills, connected text reading for grades K–1 instruction shouldn't stop there (Shanahan, 2024). Even in these early grades, students should practice their decoding and comprehension skills in grade-level text such as the student anthologies in basal reading programs (for example, HMH Into Reading or Amplify CKLA) or other common readers. Texts like student anthologies can serve as prime vehicles for moving students beyond the heavily controlled, decodable text into more authentic reading experiences. Such texts incorporate the high-frequency words learned so far and many of the phonics skills. These texts also afford the reader the chance to encounter new vocabulary, practice flexible thinking while applying the phonics skills they have learned, gain exposure to more complex sentence structure and concepts, and apply comprehension skills and strategies (Shanahan, Fisher, & Frey, 2016).

In summary, we need to provide rich reading opportunities in a variety of texts. A healthy diet of beginning reader texts, decodable texts, and selections from student anthologies will strengthen early readers and set them up for continued reading success.

Using Challenging Text for Developing Readers (Grades 2 and Up)

As in grades K–1, there is great value in using challenging connected text to engage students in second grade and up, too. In fact, the Institute of Education Sciences, in a What Works Clearinghouse report (Foorman et al., 2016), articulates that there is compelling evidence that "having students read connected text daily, both with and without constructive feedback, facilitates the development of reading accuracy, fluency, and comprehension and should begin as soon as students can identify a few words" (p. 32).

So, what types of text are considered connected texts for developing readers in second grade and beyond? Connected text at this stage of reading development includes a variety of text types, such as literary text, informational text, poetry, fables, and others. The texts may come from student anthologies, chapter books, content area textbooks, or fluency passage materials. No matter the type of text, it should help build the reader's knowledge in a variety of topics with both breadth and depth. These texts should primarily combine grade-level-difficulty texts and challenging texts (two or more grade levels above the student's current reading abilities). Developing readers may still need access to controlled text, such as a decodable reader, but they should also engage in reading grade-level text and challenging texts. So, for example, if you are a second-grade teacher, you would incorporate reading content from your core English language arts (ELA) program, science textbook, or primary sources in social studies along with decodable text to provide varied practice in grade-level and challenging texts.

In the grades K–1 section prior, I outlined several benefits of using connected text. Those same benefits apply to second grade and up, yet there are additional benefits to using connected texts for students in these grades. The additional benefits of engaging students in both grade-level text and more challenging text than they could read independently include the following:

- Developing and deepening their knowledge in a diverse range of topics and concepts that they can tap into when reading other texts (for example, reading simpler science texts on consumers and producers to prepare students for grade-level texts on the same topic)
- Increasing their access and exposure to grade-level vocabulary and sentence structure that extend beyond what conversational language would expose them to

- Building knowledge to which later learning to attach (for example, reading about the American Revolution in fifth grade as a foundation for deeper learning in eighth-grade U.S. history)

Perhaps the greatest benefit of engaging these students in more complex text is that the knowledge those texts provide gives them a significant advantage, considering that "knowledge truly is the most powerful determinant of reading comprehension" (Adams, 2010–2011, p. 10). If we want better readers, meaning readers with stronger abilities to comprehend text, we must move beyond isolated instruction on comprehension skills and strategies and build their knowledge in a range of topics. In fact, as education writer Natalie Wexler (2021) reports, "Readers who have knowledge of the topic they're reading about are better able to understand the text."

Furthermore, reading comprehension scores are highly correlated with knowledge (Willingham, 2012). So, if you want to provide the strongest foundation for the readers in your classroom, you must engage them in reading about diverse topics with grade-level or above texts that include advanced vocabulary and concepts; by doing so, they will have the cultural knowledge they need to be truly proficient readers.

Ensuring the Text Is Grade-Level Difficulty

OK, so, you are ready to engage students in reading about diverse topics with text at grade level or above, but how do you know what is grade level? There are two key factors to consider: (1) the background and interest of your students and (2) the Lexile level.

Let's start by considering the students' perspectives. A student who is enthralled with mammals and has read several books about them may be ready for more challenging texts than the grade-level text they have already been exposed to. Their interest in mammals, as well as their previous exposure to the common vocabulary and key concepts in grade-level text, will motivate them to persist through a more challenging text (Cummins, 2017). Similarly, reading a couple of easier texts on a topic can be a great way to scaffold students for more challenging texts, as they will have the foundational knowledge, vocabulary, and concepts in their background knowledge to bring to the more rigorous reading (Cervetti, Wright, & Hwang, 2016).

Another factor to consider is the students' personal backgrounds. As educators, we want all our students to have opportunities across the school year to see themselves in texts. So, selecting topics or texts that support and validate the identities, cultures, and lived experiences of your students is valuable. You can create optimal learning conditions with challenging material by finding ways to engage students in texts that they find intriguing, have prior knowledge about, have a personal connection to, or are motivated to read because of their own interest, their peers' interest, or even your enthusiasm about the content.

Now, let's consider the other element of grade-level text difficulty: Lexiles. Lexiles are a scientific approach to measuring the text complexity of reading materials (Lennon & Burdick, 2004). Lexile levels are determined by evaluating the quantitative text features. *Quantitative text features* are elements such as word length (for example, single syllable or multisyllable), sentence length and complexity, and the percentage of unfamiliar words. Basically, they are text features that are easily measured by a computer. You can use the Find a Book search tool (https://hub.lexile.com/find-a-book) to look up the Lexile level of a particular text. Booksellers such as Amazon and Barnes & Noble are adding Lexile levels to their book listings, too. If the text you are using is an article from the internet or something less formal than a published book, you can copy the material into the Text Analyzer tool (https://hub.lexile.com/text-analyzer) to calculate the Lexile level.

So, you might now be wondering, "What is the expected Lexile level for my grade level?" Fortunately, with the release of the Common Core State Standards (CCSS) for English language arts in 2010, new expectations for Lexile levels were established using a readability formula for defining grade-level reading. Each grade band has an established Lexile range for the text difficulty students are expected to be reading in class—and, ultimately, independently—by the end of the grade span. Table 1.4 shows the grade bands and their corresponding Lexile levels.

For example, if you are a fourth-grade teacher, your students should be primarily engaging in text that's within the 770–980L range. Texts at the high end of the range may require more scaffolded support, but by the end of fifth grade, students are expected to read texts at the 980L level independently.

Out of caution, I must note that Lexiles do not account for the qualitative features of a text that require a human reader, like levels of meaning, structure, language conventionality, or knowledge demands. This is why your first step may be to ensure you are using text that fits within your expected Lexile band—*but* you will also need to consider your students and the qualitative features of the text to determine whether the material is a good fit. One example is *The Hunger Games* by Suzanne Collins (2008). This book is an 810L, which suggests it would be appropriate reading for the fourth-to-fifth-grade-level band. Yet, the themes of this book, such as suffering for entertainment's sake or the intentional loss of human life, may be inappropriate for the age of the reader or may not be valued by your community. The Lexile level is a great place to start, but also consider the text itself in the context of the students you serve to be sure you are selecting appropriate materials.

Table 1.4: Grade-Level Text Difficulty Expectations

CCSS Grade Band	Lexile Expectation
K–1	N/A
2–3	450–790L
4–5	770–980L
6–8	955–1155L

Source: National Governors Association Center for Best Practices & Council of Chief State School Officers (NGA & CCSSO), 2010.

Understanding How to Use the Twenty-Five Scaffolding Strategies

Incorporating connected text into daily instruction to build proficient readers is critical (Foorman et al., 2016; Jenkins et al., 2004; National Reading Panel, 2000). The connected text should be appropriately challenging and support students in accelerating their reading growth by allowing them to practice their foundational reading skills and develop content knowledge, more advanced vocabulary, and the ability to negotiate increasingly complex sentences. However, the real challenge lies in enacting research-based practices in the classroom, where learner readiness and abilities vary. You may have students who struggle to read the most basic texts as well as students who read like high schoolers, all in the same classroom. Thinking about how to engage all of them in the same text might feel daunting.

Luckily, in the chapters that follow, I present twenty-five instructional strategies you can choose from to scaffold *all* students into grade-level text so they have the opportunity to engage with grade-level concepts, vocabulary, and sentence structures they need to learn to negotiate to be successful readers, now and in the future.

You can use these scaffolding strategies before, during, and after reading to support your students in accessing grade-level text effectively. Each scaffolding strategy includes the following six elements.

1. A simple description of the strategy
2. The value of the strategy based on research evidence
3. Considerations on when to use the strategy
4. Ideas on how to use the strategy
5. An opportunity to practice the strategy to process what you have read and apply it within your own context
6. Information on where to go for additional resources

It is important to note that you can use the scaffolding strategies I describe throughout the school day, including during:

- Core instruction (Tier 1) to support each student in accessing grade-level text
- Small-group, differentiated instruction to provide additional support for students who may require more targeted instruction (such as MLLs, students with disabilities, or students demonstrating reading difficulties)
- Intervention instruction (Tiers 2 and 3) when engaging students in text reading

I selected these scaffolding strategies for their strong research base; their ease of implementation in planning, preparation, and delivery; and their effectiveness in addressing learner variability. This menu of options allows you to consider the text—

and, most importantly, your learners—to determine which scaffolding strategies would work best. Figure 1.2 lists the scaffolding strategies, which are organized by when they are most appropriate to be executed: before reading, during reading, or after reading. Please keep in mind that some strategies can be used interchangeably, so these designations indicate when they are most commonly used. For example, the sixth before-reading strategy, making predictions, can be used prior to reading a text, but it can also be employed while reading the text by stopping at specific points within to make predictions.

Before Reading
1. Establishing a purpose for reading
2. Activating prior knowledge
3. Building background knowledge
4. Front-loading vocabulary
5. Previewing the text
6. Making predictions
7. Reading text with audio assistance
8. Reading aloud to students
9. Discussing text structure
10. Using text sets to build knowledge

During Reading
11. Engaging all students in active reading
12. Making connections
13. Asking and answering questions
14. Using graphic organizers
15. Chunking text
16. Engaging in structured academic discussion
17. Writing to learn
18. Summarizing texts using paragraph shrinking

After Reading
19. Using text-dependent questions for collaborative discussion
20. Scaffolding with partially completed graphic organizers
21. Engaging in extended writing tasks
22. Providing sentence and paragraph frames
23. Summarizing
24. Discussing with sentence frames and word banks
25. Analyzing sentence structure using syntactic awareness

Figure 1.2: Before-, during-, and after-reading scaffolding strategies.
*Visit **go.SolutionTree.com/literacy** for a free reproducible version of this figure.*

Finally, to determine which scaffolding strategies best support students in a particular text, you will need to consider how complex the text is. First, consider how challenging the text is from a quantitative perspective. Is the Lexile of the text within the grade band? Is it at the higher or lower end of the grade band? Depending on the Lexile level, students will encounter lengthier sentences and words, more unusual language or terms, and differences in text cohesiveness from sentence to sentence and paragraph to paragraph. Then, you will want to consider the qualitative features of the text that may make it challenging. The CCSS for English language arts (NGA & CCSSO, 2010) include four domains for analyzing the qualitative complexity of text: (1) levels of meaning or purpose, (2) structure, (3) language conventionality and clarity, and (4) knowledge demands. Figure 1.3 provides questions you can consider when identifying the complexity demands of a text.

Levels of Meaning or Purpose	Structure
• **Single level or multiple levels of meaning?** Does the literary text have a single level of meaning, or does it have multiple levels (such as satires)? • **Stated or unstated purpose?** Does the informational text explicitly state the purpose, or is the purpose implicit, hidden, or obscure?	• **Simple or complex?** Does the literary text flow in a chronological order, or does it include flashbacks, flashforwards, multiple points of view, and so on? • **Conventional or unusual?** Does the informational text use conventional traits for the genre or topic, or does it use traits that are unique to the content or discipline? • **Essential or nonessential visuals?** Are the graphics simple and unnecessary or merely supplemental to the text, or do they contain additional information that's essential to understanding it?
Language Conventionality and Clarity	**Knowledge Demands**
• **Literal or figurative?** Does the text rely on literal, clear, everyday language, or does it rely on figurative, ironic, ambiguous, archaic, or unfamiliar discipline-specific language?	• **Simple or complex theme?** Does it have a simple or complex theme? • **Single theme or multiple themes?** Does it have one theme or multiple themes? • **Unusual or everyday experiences?** Does the text contain common everyday experiences or experiences that are likely vastly different from the reader's? • **Single perspective or multiple perspectives?** Does the text represent a single perspective or multiple perspectives? Are the perspectives similar or in opposition to the reader's?

Figure 1.3: Four qualitative domains of complex text.

By thinking about the complexity of the text—both its quantitative and qualitative features—you can identify the strategies that will be most needed in a particular text. For example, if a text has a high frequency of unknown words in an unfamiliar context for the students, building background knowledge and front-loading vocabulary before reading the text would be helpful. To facilitate this process, there is a key at the beginning of each strategy that recommends which complexity elements the scaffolding strategy might best address. Figure 1.4 is an example of how this key will look. In this example, High Lexile, Levels of Meaning, and Knowledge Demands are bolded, indicating that this strategy addresses these elements.

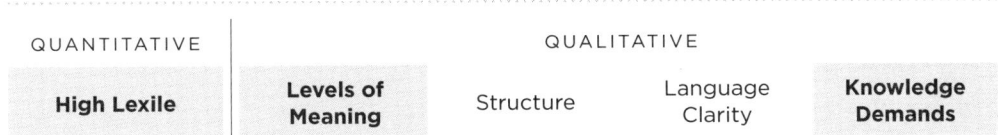

Figure 1.4: Challenging text elements feature.

Before Reading

1. Establishing a purpose for reading

2. Activating prior knowledge

3. Building background knowledge

4. Front-loading vocabulary

5. Previewing the text

6. Making predictions

7. Reading text with audio assistance

8. Reading aloud to students

9. Discussing text structure

10. Using text sets to build knowledge

Chapter Two

Scaffolding Strategies to Use Before Reading

In this chapter, you will find ten before-reading scaffolding strategies for your consideration and planning purposes. Of these ten strategies, strategy 1 is the only one that should be used no matter the text. The research is compellingly clear that when teachers establish a clear purpose for the learning activity, students learn at higher levels, so you should always establish the purpose before reading the text (Fraser, Walberg, Welch, & Hattie, 1987; Samuels & Dahl, 1975). Using the other strategies will depend on the content and design of the text as well as what your learners are bringing to the text. For example, if they have deep prior knowledge about the topic at hand, there is less of a need to front-load the vocabulary or build background knowledge; but if the structure of the text is unusual, it is likely beneficial to discuss the text structure prior to reading. This is where your professional judgment as an educator comes into play, as you know your students best.

As you select which strategies to use with a particular text, you can refer to these general categories to aid your selection.

- **Prior knowledge:** If most students have some knowledge of the topic in the text, then you may want to consider using these strategies.
    - *Strategy 2*—Activating prior knowledge
    - *Strategy 6*—Making predictions
- **Limited knowledge:** If the content is relatively unknown to the students, then these strategies might be most appropriate.
    - *Strategy 3*—Building background knowledge
    - *Strategy 4*—Front-loading vocabulary

- *Strategy 7*—Reading text with audio assistance
- *Strategy 8*—Reading aloud to students
- *Strategy 10*—Using text sets to build knowledge

○ **Organization of the text:** If the layout or design of the text may challenge students due to its novelty, orientation, or other feature, then you may want to consider using one of these strategies.

- *Strategy 5*—Previewing the text
- *Strategy 9*—Discussing text structure

Scaffolding Strategy 1: Establishing a Purpose for Reading

QUANTITATIVE	QUALITATIVE			
High Lexile	Levels of Meaning	Structure	Language Clarity	Knowledge Demands

In this strategy, the teacher clearly communicates at the beginning of the lesson, and reinforces throughout, the lesson's learning intentions and success criteria that describe the skills and knowledge that students need to learn.

Why It Matters

Establishing a purpose for reading prior to the lesson and revisiting it throughout the lesson are powerful, as doing so clarifies for students what the focus of the lesson is and what is expected of them. Students are more likely to meet the desired intentions of the lesson when teachers clearly communicate the success criteria and intended learning gains (Fisher et al., 2024; Titsworth, Mazer, Goodboy, Bolkan, & Myers, 2015).

What to Consider Before Implementing

As you establish a purpose for reading, ensure it's aligned to your core standards and you communicate it in student-friendly language. After you communicate the expectation, check for understanding by asking students to articulate what they are learning, why they are learning it, and how they will know they learned it. You can do this by having students talk with a partner about the learning intentions and success criteria while you monitor their understanding of the established purpose.

You will also want to revisit the purpose throughout the lesson, not just at the beginning. Use the purpose as an anchor for the lesson that you refer to and connect with across the learning so that students have a consistent reminder of what they are doing and why and can monitor their progress. Furthermore, by being clear about the purpose of the learning, you can reduce student apprehension, especially for developing readers, and improve their processing of information, yielding higher levels of comprehension (Chesebro & McCroskey, 2001).

> **TEACHER TIP**
>
> As you present the purpose of the lesson, be sure to make the content comprehensible for your MLLs. This might include gesturing, showing images that support the content, using common vocabulary from one lesson to the next for consistency, or affording students the opportunity to talk with one another to process together. Whatever you do, the goal is to be sure that every student knows the purpose of the lesson.

How to Implement the Strategy

By establishing a purpose before reading, you are clueing your students in on exactly what you want them to focus their attention on. So, let's say you are going to read the fable "The Tortoise and the Hare" with the primary intention of working on the second-grade CCSS standard for reading that states, "Recount stories, including fables and folktales from diverse cultures, and determine their central message, lesson, or moral" (ELA-Literacy.RL.2.2). Communicate the lesson's purpose to students at the beginning of the lesson. For example, you might say, "Our learning intention for reading is to recount the story of 'The Tortoise and the Hare' and identify the lesson of the story. We will do so by telling the story to a partner using a story map and citing evidence to support our lesson conclusion."

Figure 2.1 shows the established purpose using student-friendly learning intentions and success criteria. By explicitly stating what students will be learning (learning intention) and how they will know if they learned it (success criteria), you establish the purpose for reading and give them a road map to the learning destination ahead.

Learning Intentions	Success Criteria
I can recount the story of "The Tortoise and the Hare."	I will recount the story of "The Tortoise and the Hare" to a partner using a story map.
I can identify the lesson of the story.	I can provide evidence to support what I think is the lesson of the story.

Figure 2.1: Learning intentions and success criteria for "The Tortoise and the Hare."

You should then revisit the purpose for reading at least once during the reading of the text but ideally twice, at about halfway through and as the lesson wraps up, to consistently reiterate the purpose and to bring the students' attention back to the goal.

> **TEACHER TIP**
>
> The language you use to articulate the purpose needs to be student friendly, and be sure to clearly communicate what it looks like to successfully achieve the learning intentions by the end of the lesson.

The following is an example of what teacher scripting might sound like for this scaffolding strategy.

Teacher: *Our learning intention for today is "I can recount the story of 'The Tortoise and the Hare.'" Turn to your elbow partner and tell them what we will be focusing on for our reading time today.*

[Students turn to their partners and talk about what it means to recount a story.]

Teacher: [Calls the class back together.] *Now, Jonah, what did you and Melanie share?*

Jonah: *It means we have to tell the story in our own words, right?*

Teacher: *Exactly! We're going to retell the story in our own words. And to help us do that effectively, we have our success criteria that says, "I will recount the story of 'The Tortoise and the Hare' to a partner using a story map."*

[Teacher points to the words *story map* on the board.]

Teacher: *Now, who can remind us what a story map is?*

[A student raises their hand.]

Student: *It's like a visual organizer that helps us understand the key elements of a story, like the characters, setting, problem, and solution.*

Teacher: *That's right! So today, as we recount the story of "The Tortoise and the Hare" to our partners, we'll use our story maps to make sure we include all the important details.*

How to Practice the Strategy

Choose a text and at least one grade-level standard. Write the learning intentions and then the success criteria you would use to establish the purpose for reading in figure 2.2. Keep the language as simple and student friendly as possible.

Learning Intentions	Success Criteria

*Figure 2.2: Learning intentions and success criteria used to establish a purpose for reading. Visit **go.SolutionTree.com/literacy** for a free reproducible version of this figure.*

For more on establishing a purpose for reading, including examples across content areas, please visit the additional resources online (**go.SolutionTree.com/literacy**).

Scaffolding Strategy 2: Activating Prior Knowledge

QUANTITATIVE	QUALITATIVE			
High Lexile	**Levels of Meaning**	Structure	Language Clarity	**Knowledge Demands**

In this strategy, teachers activate students' prior knowledge or lived experience on the topic at hand to create connections between students' prior knowledge and the new learning.

Why It Matters

When students have some prior knowledge on a topic, activating that knowledge can help students connect the new learning with their existing knowledge, as it gives the new knowledge a place in the brain to attach it to (Hattan, Alexander, & Lupo, 2024; McCarthy & McNamara, 2021); thus, it increases the likelihood that the students retain the information in their long-term memory. Good readers bring in their world of knowledge to help them make sense of the text or make inferences, whereas developing readers are unlikely to do so. By using this strategy, you can help students build this skill (Pressley & Afflerbach, 1995).

What to Consider Before Implementing

To activate prior knowledge, students need to have already learned or experienced something related to the topic at hand. If you are introducing a topic that your students have limited or no prior experience with, then this will not be an effective strategy. For example, when I taught in Alaska, there was a story about students who lived in the desert in New Mexico. My students collectively had very little, if any, knowledge of the desert, so if I had tried to activate their prior knowledge, it would not have been a productive use of time. But, when I taught in Utah, student knowledge of the desert would be expected given that they live in the desert. Knowledge matters!

How to Implement the Strategy

There are numerous ways to activate students' prior knowledge. The following are a few examples, though not an exhaustive list, of the different ways to activate students' prior knowledge. When selecting a strategy to help activate prior knowledge, the general rule of thumb is to use any instructional tactic that allows students to consider what they already know about the topic prior to engaging in the new learning. It is important to keep this part of the lesson brief, about three to five minutes, as the goal is to spend most of the time engaging in the new learning—not spending too much time reviewing what students already know. The bulk of the lesson should be focused on the new learning.

- Organizers filled out in advance, such as a K-W-L (What I Know-What I Want to Know-What I Learned) chart, can help. (See figure 2.3 for an example.) Asking students what they know about the topic at hand prior to engaging in the content helps students be ready to make connections with the new content, and it can serve as a formative assessment practice for the teacher to identify already known ideas as well as potential misconceptions. Using a K-W-L chart can activate students' background knowledge by asking them what they already *know* about the topic, what they *want* to learn, and what they have already *learned* about it. During and after reading, you can return to the chart and clear up any misconceptions that students may have initially expressed.

- Anticipation-reaction guides contain a list of statements about the topic at hand for students to respond to before and after reading. They are designed as a series of usually four to six statements related to the key concepts or themes of the learning that students mark as *agree* or *disagree* (or *true* or *false*). (See figure 2.4 for an example.) Before the lesson, students evaluate each statement based on their current knowledge. During or after the lesson, students return to the same statements and decide if they want to adjust any of their answers based on what they have learned. You can even encourage them to cite text evidence to support their opinion.

- You can also use visuals to activate students' prior knowledge. For example, if students are going to learn about similarities and differences between reptiles and birds, you might display examples of commonly known reptiles and birds to jump-start their thinking.

Butterflies		
What I Know	**What I Want to Know**	**What I Learned**
• Have colorful wings • Fly • Migrate • Were once caterpillars	• What do they eat? • How long does it take for a caterpillar to change into a butterfly? • How long do they live?	• Use their proboscis to drink nectar from flowers • Transform from a larva to a butterfly after four weeks • Live anywhere from one to two weeks to several months • Are insects • Taste with their feet

Figure 2.3: Sample K-W-L chart for the topic of butterflies.

TEACHER TIP

For an MLL, scaffolding a text-heavy chart, such as a K-W-L, by adding pictures or drawings can help make the content more comprehensible. So, if the chart includes "have colorful wings," you could draw a butterfly wing that has many colors. Simple drawings can reduce the linguistic demands and support the MLL in being able to use the chart more effectively.

Statement	Agree	Disagree	Before Reading	After Reading
Butterflies taste with their antennae.		✓	They taste with their mouths.	They taste with their feet. Page 24
The life cycle of a butterfly is egg *to* caterpillar *to* butterfly.				
The life span of all butterflies is one to two weeks.				

Figure 2.4: Sample anticipation-reaction guide for butterflies.

The following is an example of what teacher scripting might sound like for this scaffolding strategy.

[Throughout the lesson, the teacher keeps a keen eye on the K-W-L chart, ready to engage students in reflective moments.]

Teacher: *All right, class, let's take a quick break from our reading. I want everyone to look at our K-W-L chart and think about what new information we've gathered so far about "The Tortoise and the Hare." Take a moment to jot down any new insights or connections you've made.*

[Students grab their pencils and eagerly add to the L section of the chart, discussing their observations with their peers.]

Teacher: *Excellent! I see some great additions to our chart. It's wonderful to see how our understanding is growing as we delve deeper into the story.*

[Later in the lesson, the teacher pauses again to revisit the K-W-L chart.]

Teacher: *All right, class, let's check in with our K-W-L chart one more time before we wrap up. Take a moment to reflect on what we've learned today and how it connects to what we already knew.*

[Students eagerly share their thoughts, pointing out new details they've discovered and drawing connections to their prior knowledge.]

Teacher: *Fantastic! I'm so proud of all the connections you've made today. It's clear that our prior knowledge has helped us better understand the story of "The Tortoise and the Hare."*

[As the lesson comes to a close, the teacher gathers students for a final discussion.]

Teacher: *Before we finish for the day, let's take a moment to reflect on how our understanding of "The Tortoise and the Hare" has evolved. What are some key insights we've gained, and how do they deepen our understanding of the story?*

[Students eagerly share their reflections, discussing the new perspectives they've gained and the connections they've made.]

How to Practice the Strategy

Select a text on a topic that your students likely already know something about. Describe how you might use a K-W-L chart, anticipation-reaction guide, visuals, or another tool to activate your students' prior knowledge about the topic. Be sure to consider how you will bring them back to the chart or other visuals throughout the lesson to actively foster new connections to their prior knowledge and the new material.

For more on activating prior knowledge, including more about K-W-L, please access the additional resources online (**go.SolutionTree.com/literacy**).

Scaffolding Strategy 3: Building Background Knowledge

QUANTITATIVE	QUALITATIVE			
High Lexile	**Levels of Meaning**	Structure	Language Clarity	**Knowledge Demands**

With this strategy, teachers identify the essential concepts, experiences, information, and text structures that may prevent or undermine the students' ability to comprehend the text at hand, and they learn to front-load the readers with that knowledge to mediate the difficulty (Brody, 2001).

Why It Matters

In their book, *Make It Stick: The Science of Successful Learning*, Peter C. Brown, Henry L. Roediger, and Mark A. McDaniel (2014) write, "All new learning requires a foundation of prior knowledge" (p. 5). Numerous studies have shown the influential role that background knowledge plays in reading comprehension (Alexander, Kulikowich, & Schulze, 1994; Shapiro, 2004; Smith, Snow, Serry, & Hammond, 2021). So, if you are introducing or engaging in a concept that is relatively unknown to your students, this is the perfect time to provide them with a base of essential knowledge, such as key concepts or vocabulary, that they will need to know to effectively access the text and make meaning from it. After all, it makes sense that students will need some base knowledge about the topic to comprehend a text about it.

Unlike in strategy 2 (activating prior knowledge), teachers should use this strategy when students have little to no previous understanding of the concepts that they will encounter. Additionally, by taking the time to build background knowledge relevant to the text, you can greatly reduce the risk of developing readers misunderstanding the text.

What to Consider Before Implementing

In contrast to activating prior knowledge, building background knowledge is not about teasing out what students already know (which would likely include misconceptions) but rather seeding accurate details about the key concepts or elements to make the text more comprehensible. For example, by building background knowledge prior to reading, you can assist readers in deciphering words with multiple potential meanings. This is especially true for informational text, as it tends to incorporate a greater volume of vocabulary and concepts unknown to the student (Price, Bradley, & Smith, 2012). So, if the class is about to begin a text about the vampire bat, introducing bats will help the reader choose the right conception of the term. The word *bat* has over a dozen potential definitions and uses. If you were to say to your class, "Today we are going to read a text about bats," one student might be thinking of a baseball bat, while another may be thinking of the mammal—your intended meaning. By simply showing a picture of the type of bat you'll be reading about, you can quickly avoid any potential misunderstandings.

Similarly, introducing figurative language, such as metaphors or idioms, can be helpful to support the students' understanding of the text. Let's say the text you are reading is about a young girl acting in her first play, and her friend says, "Break a leg!" right before she goes on stage to perform. Some students might take this literally and be mightily confused about why her friend would say such a thing. Instead, you can mitigate this misunderstanding and avoid confused looks from your students by front-loading that idiomatic phrase.

Additionally, consider if there are key concepts or vocabulary that are new to your students and provide a brief introduction to them. This will allow them to leverage that new learning and consolidate it into the reading process, thereby increasing their comprehension of the new information.

TEACHER TIP

It is essential to more explicitly attend to idiomatic and other types of figurative language for MLLs (Palmer, Shackelford, Miller, & Leclere, 2006). Consider the idiomatic phrase *raining cats and dogs* and imagine how a student might interpret it literally. Your intended meaning was a bit different, right? As you preview a text prior to reading it with your class, look for those moments where figurative language may distract or disrupt students' understanding and plan for how you will address their misunderstandings quickly and efficiently.

How to Implement the Strategy

Given the influence of background knowledge on reading comprehension, taking time prior to reading a text to introduce concepts that are unknown to the reader will make the reading experience infinitely more productive. Here are four simple ideas for building background knowledge.

1. Use video to provide an indirect yet visual experience of the information students will encounter.
2. Explicitly teach key concepts, vocabulary, or figurative language that is essential to comprehending the text.
3. Read simpler texts about the topic (Arfé, Mason, & Fajardo, 2018).
4. Compare and contrast the new concept with a concept the students already know.

To illustrate this, let's use a standard from the Next Generation Science Standards (NGSS Lead States, 2013): "Read texts and use media to determine patterns in behavior of parents and offspring that help offspring survive" (1-LS1-2). Figure 2.5 demonstrates what each of these four techniques might look like in the classroom.

Technique	Implementation
Use Multimedia	Select a video that shows how baby birds chirp to indicate to their parents that they are hungry and how the parent responds by bringing them food.
Front-Load Key Vocabulary or Concepts	Front-load the words *survival*, *parent*, *offspring*, and *similar*. (See figure 2.8, page 35, for an explicit instructional routine for front-loading vocabulary.)
Start With Simpler Texts	Find one or two beginning readers or simple picture books that explore the behaviors of birds and their offspring that help the offspring survive. Read those texts to or with the students to establish a base foundation of knowledge.
Compare and Contrast to Already Known Ideas	Engage the students in a discussion and use a graphic organizer to take notes on how their parents help them survive (for example, by feeding them, clothing them, and keeping them safe). Have them look for similarities as they read about how their parents help them survive and how birds help their offspring survive. Refer to the graphic organizer for an ongoing compare-and-contrast opportunity during text reading. (See strategy 14, page 84, for more information on using graphic organizers.)

Figure 2.5: Techniques for building background knowledge.

How to Practice the Strategy

Select a science or social studies text that your students will be reading. Use the template in figure 2.6 to think through how you could use these techniques to build their background knowledge to prepare them for reading the chosen text. Remember, you do not need to use all these strategies, but thinking through each of them may help you select the one or two that may be most fitting for the text your students will encounter.

Technique	How You Might Use It
Use Multimedia	
Front-Load Key Vocabulary or Concepts	
Start With Simpler Texts	
Compare and Contrast to Already Known Ideas	

Figure 2.6: *Planning tool for building background knowledge.*

Visit go.SolutionTree.com/literacy for a free reproducible version of this figure.

For more on building background knowledge, including when supporting MLLs, please access the additional resources online (**go.SolutionTree.com/literacy**).

Scaffolding Strategy 4: Front-loading Vocabulary

QUANTITATIVE	QUALITATIVE			
High Lexile	**Levels of Meaning**	Structure	Language Clarity	**Knowledge Demands**

In this strategy, to support students' understanding, teachers explicitly front-load high-utility and key terms students will need to know to meaningfully interpret the text before they encounter the new vocabulary.

Why It Matters

A critical factor on whether a student will be able to comprehend a text is vocabulary knowledge (August, Carlo, Dressler, & Snow, 2005; Baumann, 2009; Chall, Jacobs, & Baldwin, 1990; Cunningham & Stanovich, 1997; Kintsch, 1998; Kintsch & van Dijk, 1978; Mancilla-Martinez & Lesaux, 2010). When students understand the essential vocabulary in a text, they are more likely to be able to comprehend the text at high levels. Decoding the words alone is insufficient for aiding reading comprehension. Students need to know the meaning of most words in the text to successfully negotiate its meaning. Unfortunately, developing readers are also likely to have a less robust base vocabulary. Taking time to front-load, or preteach, key vocabulary to developing readers is a powerful strategy for improving students' understanding of the text they'll be reading.

What to Consider Before Implementing

Selecting the words to teach is the most important step of front-loading vocabulary apart from using an explicit vocabulary instruction routine (but we will get to that in a moment). You don't want to choose words that most of your students already know or ones that are already defined in the text (for example, "calabash, a small pumpkin"). You want to choose words that have *high utility*, or have use well beyond that day's reading passage, and are critical to comprehending the text.

A useful way to identify which words you should explicitly teach is Isabel L. Beck, Margaret G. McKeown, and Linda Kucan's (2013) three tiers of vocabulary, as they describe in their book *Bringing Words to Life*. In this model, words are categorized into one of three tiers (see figure 2.7).

Three Tiers of Vocabulary Words	Examples
Tier 1: Everyday words	*cup, ball, nose*
Tier 2: High-utility words	*attention, concerning, compare*
Tier 3: Content-specific words	*metamorphosis, chrysalis, quadrilateral*

Figure 2.7: Three tiers of vocabulary words.

Tier 1 words are very common words used in daily conversation that most of your students will know. Note that if you have any developing readers or MLLs, you may need to explicitly front-load Tier 1 words, too. Your English language development small-group time can be an optimal opportunity to do so. *Tier 2 words* are those words that students will encounter frequently in text, now and in the future. They are words that are useful across contexts, like *analyze, describe, concerned, dependent*, or *survive*. *Tier 3 words* are described as content- or discipline-specific words. These are words that students will generally only encounter within content-specific domains, like *photosynthesis* in a science text or *rhombus* in mathematics. You will also need to explicitly teach Tier 3 words when the content calls for it.

Be mindful of the cognitive limitations of the human brain by restricting your daily vocabulary instruction to no more than two to three words per selection (Beck et al., 2002). Introducing too many words can make it too challenging to retain the words and their meanings. Instead, explicitly teach two to three new words a day while incorporating activities that provide a cumulative review of all the words you taught across the week. This makes it more likely for words to move from short-term to long-term memory for later use and retrieval (Beck et al., 2002).

Many comprehensive core ELA programs will select the key vocabulary they recommend for instruction. Although this can be helpful, we must remember that those words were selected for the average student, and our class of students may not be "average." You know your students best, so be ready to make sound instructional decisions about which words they may need to best access the reading material.

> **TEACHER TIP**
>
> As you use your ELA core program, look for how it provides recommendations for how to support MLLs in accessing the language demands of the text. Often, core programs will provide suggestions and strategies in the text for how to support your MLLs. These recommendations can be great time savers for you.

Also, keep in mind that you can incorporate incidental vocabulary learning into the lesson, too. Incidental vocabulary learning happens as students listen to read alouds, engage in oral language experiences, and read on their own. These are great opportunities to incorporate "teachable moments," such as quickly teaching a word that you didn't anticipate would cause your students to struggle or providing a word or phrase that is a synonym to an unknown word being used at the point of instruction. For example, if you are reading along and the text mentions a "bongo," you might quickly explain, "A bongo is like a small drum," and then keep reading. This allows you to support additional vocabulary needs without taking too much instruction time or overburdening the students' cognitive abilities.

How to Implement the Strategy

Now that you know what to consider when selecting which words to explicitly teach, you need an explicit vocabulary routine that you can use consistently when teaching your students new words. For you, using an instructional routine allows you to quickly prepare and execute a powerful strategy for scaffolding students with words that they would find challenging in the text and that would likely hinder their comprehension. For the students, using an instructional routine allows them to free up cognitive space to focus on the new learning and not the *how* of the lesson. They don't have to think about how you are delivering the lesson or what may be coming next because they will already know, and that maximizes the amount of cognitive bandwidth they have available for word learning.

An explicit vocabulary routine has several critical components that you can execute day after day when teaching new words. According to reading researchers (Armbruster, Lehr, & Osborn, 2001; Beck et al., 2002; National Reading Panel, 2000; Stahl & Fairbanks, 1986), essential elements of an effective vocabulary instruction routine include the following:

- A student-friendly definition (not necessarily a dictionary definition)
- Use of the target word in context with examples and nonexamples
- A nonlinguistic representation of the word (such as an image, object, or gesture)
- Ample opportunity to practice saying the word correctly
- A check for understanding of the word's meaning

An example of an explicit vocabulary instruction routine for the word *attention* is provided in figure 2.8. This word is used in Peggy Rathmann's (1995) children's picture book, *Officer Buckle and Gloria*, to describe the behavior of Gloria, the police dog, and her interactions with Officer Buckle.

Explicit Routine Element	Teacher Script
Establish Purpose	**Teacher:** *To help us prepare for reading our story today, we will learn a few of the vocabulary words that will help us to better understand the text. You will practice saying, reading, and using the word to deepen your understanding of the new word.*
Introduce the Word in Context	**Teacher:** *[Displays the word* attention *and a picture of a student using a crosswalk with the help of a crossing guard.] When you cross the street by looking both ways and follow the directions of the crossing guard, you are showing attention.*
Practice *See and Say*	**Teacher:** *Our word is* attention. *What's the word?* **Students:** *[Chorally respond.] Attention.* **Teacher:** *Say "attention" to the clock.* **Students:** *[Chorally respond and look at the clock.] Attention.* **Teacher:** *Say "attention" to your elbow.* **Students:** *[Chorally respond and look at their elbows.] Attention.* **Teacher:** *Say "attention" to the ceiling.*

Figure 2.8: Explicit vocabulary instruction routine for attention.

continued →

Explicit Routine Element	Teacher Script
	Students: [Chorally respond and look up at the ceiling.] Attention. **Teacher:** Now, how many syllables are in the word attention? Let's tap it out. **Students:** [Clap three times.] At-ten-tion. Three! **Teacher:** Yes, there are three syllables. At-ten-tion. **Cognates (if there are native Spanish-speaking students)** **Teacher:** The word attention has a cognate—a word that sounds similar—in Spanish. The word attention in Spanish is atención. What's the Spanish word for attention? **Students:** Atención. **Affixes and Roots** **Teacher:** The word attention has other forms, so your knowledge of attention will help you interpret the meaning of similar words, like attend, attendant, attentiveness, inattentiveness, attentive, inattentive, attentively, inattentively. (These words should be visually displayed.)
Define in Student-Friendly Language	**Teacher:** Attention is when you carefully listen to, look at, or think about someone or something.
Provide Another Example in Context	**Teacher:** So, in the classroom, you would show that you are paying attention by looking at your teacher and listening to what they are saying, or you are paying attention when you are thinking about what the teacher is asking you to do. Now, show me what it would look like to demonstrate you are paying attention. [Students use their bodies to show that they are looking at the teacher and giving them their full attention.] **Teacher:** Oh, I love how Marcus is looking at me; he has his hands to himself, and all his attention is on me. And Josie, she is sitting up and leaning toward me, and she has her eyes on me. I can tell she is really paying attention.
Practice the Word With Yes-No Statements	**Teacher:** Now, to check your understanding of the word attention, I am going to read some sentences. If I use the word attention correctly, then say "attention" and give me a thumbs-up. If I don't use it correctly, make an X with your arms. Let's try it. You are showing that you are paying attention when you sit up straight, look at the teacher, and have your hands to yourself. **Students:** [Put their thumbs up.] Attention. **Teacher:** If there was a dog running around in the classroom, then you might have a hard time paying attention. **Students:** [Put their thumbs up.] Attention.

	Teacher: *If you were playing a game while the principal asked you to clean up your mess, you would be showing attention.* [Students make an X with their arms.] **Teacher:** *If you were reading a book and kept your eyes on the text, even though someone next to you dropped something, you would be paying attention.* **Students:** *[Put their thumbs up.] Attention.*
Check for Understanding With Structured Student Talk	**Teacher:** *OK, it's your turn to use the word* attention *in a sentence. Use this sentence starter to share your sentence: "If I were paying attention in class, I would be . . ."* [Students turn to a partner and use the sentence starter to provide an example sentence that shows their understanding of the word attention.] **Student 1:** *If I were paying attention in class, I would be ignoring a friend trying to talk to me.* **Student 2:** *If I were paying attention in class, I would be doing what the teacher asked me to do.*
Wrap Up	**Teacher:** *So, our word is* attention. *What's the word?* **Students:** *Attention.* **Teacher:** *Now, let's see how attention is used in our story.*

How to Practice the Strategy

Choose two to three words from a challenging text that your students will be reading soon. To prepare to teach those words, use the template for the explicit vocabulary instruction routine (see figure 2.9) or draw a line down the middle of a piece of paper to make a two-column chart for recording. Remember to be thoughtful about which words you choose, as you want them to be words that students need for the long-term and will encounter time and time again across a variety of texts. See figure 2.9 for an overview of the steps in the explicit vocabulary instruction routine and some teacher tips to keep in mind.

Routine	Teacher Tips
Step 1: Establish Purpose What are the learning intentions and success criteria for the lesson?	• Inform students what they will be learning and why, including what success will look like.
Step 2: Introduce the Word in Context What visuals, realia, or gestures will you use to provide a nonlinguistic representation of the word?	• Find a picture or object or create a gesture to help students have a nonlinguistic representation of the word. • Display the word. • Provide an example of the word in context.

Figure 2.9: Teacher tips for using the explicit vocabulary instruction routine.

continued →

Routine	Teacher Tips
Step 3: Practice *See and Say* What affixes, roots, or other forms and cognates are possible?	• Have students practice saying the word multiple times (for example, to the clock, to their shoe, to their neighbor). • Have students identify the number of syllables. • Check for cognates, if available, to support MLLs. • Have students look for and identify roots and affixes, if available.
Step 4: Define in Student-Friendly Language What words do students already know that you could use to define the new vocabulary word?	• Share a student-friendly definition.
Step 5: Provide Another Example in Context What is another context the students might encounter the word in?	• Share another example of the vocabulary word in a different context than previously used.
Step 6: Practice the Word With Yes-No Statements How can you demonstrate correct and incorrect use of the vocabulary word?	• Provide examples and nonexamples of the word in context and ask students to determine whether you are using the word correctly or incorrectly. • Determine what hand gestures or verbal cues you want students to use.
Step 7: Check for Understanding With Structured Student Talk What sentence starter or frame do you want students to use? How will you formatively assess their understanding?	• Provide students with a sentence frame or starter to demonstrate their understanding of the word.
Step 8: Wrap Up How will you revisit the established purpose?	• Repeat the word and have students repeat it, too.

*Visit **go.SolutionTree.com/literacy** for a free reproducible version of this figure.*

For more on front-loading vocabulary, including inspiration for creating student-friendly definitions, please access the additional resources online (**go.SolutionTree.com/literacy**).

Scaffolding Strategy 5: Previewing the Text

QUANTITATIVE	QUALITATIVE			
High Lexile	Levels of Meaning	**Structure**	Language Clarity	**Knowledge Demands**

In this strategy, students survey a text to explore what it has to offer and to notice key elements of the text (such as illustrations, headings and subheadings, and organization) without reading it word for word, all while creating a mental map of the text. This provides developing readers with background knowledge they can bring to the text to increase their comprehension along the way.

Why It Matters

Spending a few minutes previewing before jumping into reading the text can aid students' comprehension of the text (Graves, Cooke, & Laberge, 1983). Taking time to preview the text prior to reading and looking for various features and information that will be explored in more depth afford students the opportunity to activate their prior knowledge (see strategy 2, page 25) on the topic as well as consider the purpose (see strategy 1, page 22) of the text. This is particularly useful for developing readers, as they are often less experienced with text than other students and may not know the common features or aspects to expect.

What to Consider Before Implementing

The first step in this strategy is to identify if the text is literary or informational text, as that will impact the approach to the preview. If the text is literary, then looking at things like the title, illustrations, and chapter headings can be valuable. If the text is informational, then looking at the headings and subheadings, illustrations, captions, and other text features can add value. Being explicit with students about the type of text and which features they may want to examine depending on the type of text is extremely important as you build their independence in being able to use this strategy without prompting.

As an adult, you likely preview a text without even thinking about it. For example, if you were at a bookstore or library and picked up a book, you would likely look at the cover and then flip through the pages, looking at the chapters or images, or turn to the back of the book to read the summary. By previewing the book, you get a sense of what the text is going to be like and how you may need to approach it. If it is informational, you may look to see if there is an index to help you pinpoint the specific information you are looking for, or you may look to see if it has some useful visuals to support the written text, or you may consider what information you already know about the topic based on what you are seeing. If it is literary, you may look at the chapter titles—

how many there are or even how many pages are in a chapter (at least that is something I do, as I struggle to stay engaged with books with long chapters).

By modeling how to preview a text, we empower students with a strategy that they will use for years to come: When they encounter a new text, they will be able to identify how they might best approach the materials and consider what prior knowledge they might bring to bear or what their purpose for engaging in that text might be, such as to learn something new, gain information, or entertain (Ajideh, 2006; Alfaki & Siddiek, 2013; Ringler & Weber, 1984).

How to Implement the Strategy

To preview a text, there are specific elements you will want to consider (depending on the text).

- The title, including titles of visual aids
- Any opening information about the author
- The first sentence in each paragraph
- The headings and subheadings
- The illustrations, diagrams, graphs, tables, photos, or other visuals
- Any italicized, bolded, or highlighted words
- Any comprehension questions or related learning activities that follow the text

The elements of a text, like those in the preceding list, will vary—especially between informational and literary texts, which often differ in their common text features—but this very quickly becomes a go-to strategy for students that is easily adaptable to any text. As you preview a new text for your students, you can determine if there are other features that might be useful to draw their attention to, but this list will give you a good start.

An evidence-based instruction routine you can teach your students to guide them in previewing text is THIEVES (Liff Manz, 2002). *THIEVES*—which stands for **T**itle, **H**eadings, **I**ntroduction, **E**very first sentence in a paragraph, **V**isuals and vocabulary, **E**nd-of-text questions, and **S**ummary—is a mnemonic that students can use to remember to work their way through a simple process for previewing a text that involves "stealing" information from key text elements (see figure 2.10).

In introducing this routine, teach the students what each letter in THIEVES stands for and practice using those elements with students to question how that information may help them understand what the text will be about. With practice, this routine can become automatic for your students to bring to any new text. To further enhance this routine, you may want to consider creating an anchor chart or a bookmark of the seven elements in order to provide students with a quick visual cue as they work to master this routine (see figure 2.11).

Scaffolding Strategies to Use Before Reading | 41

THIEVES Element	Sample Questions to Ask Myself
Title	What is the title? What is my prior knowledge on this topic?
Headings	How is the information divided? What are the smaller topics in the text?
Introduction	What information does the introduction provide?
Every first sentence in a paragraph	What do I think the selection is going to be about based on the first sentence of each paragraph?
Visuals and vocabulary	What information do the visuals add? Are there important words in bold or italics or any that are highlighted? Do I know what those words mean?
End-of-text questions	What do the questions ask me to know? Given the questions, what do I think the reading will be about?
Summary	What do I think the main idea will be?

Figure 2.10: THIEVES mnemonic.

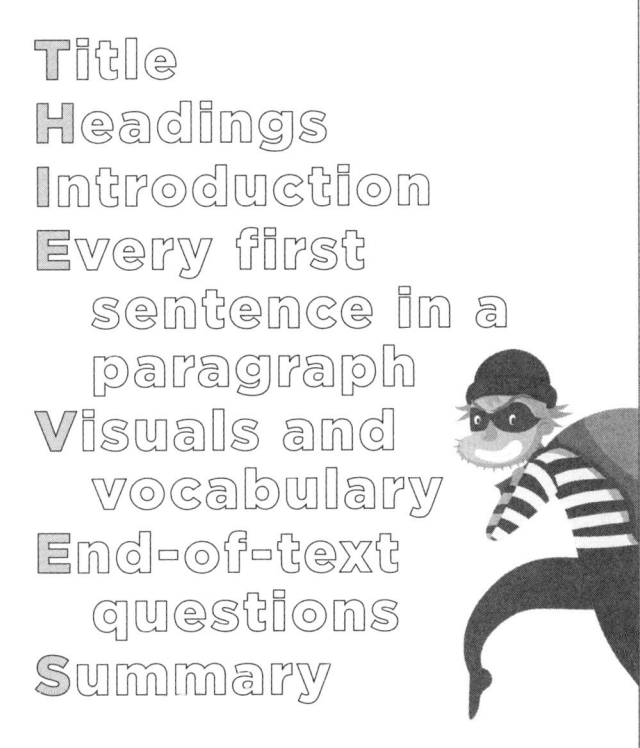

Figure 2.11: THIEVES anchor chart.

> **TEACHER TIP**
>
> Mnemonics can provide a strong anchor for MLLs as they work to read and comprehend the text by making it easier for them to process and recall a procedure. They also help make a process easier to break down into manageable chunks and support automatic retrieval over time with practice (Brown et al., 2014).

How to Practice the Strategy

Practice using the THIEVES routine with an upcoming reading selection for your class. Go through the seven elements of THIEVES and consider any other questions you would add to the sample questions provided. Then, add them to figure 2.12.

THIEVES Element	Sample Questions to Ask Myself	Other Questions I Could Ask
Title	What is the title? What is my prior knowledge on this topic?	
Headings	How is the information divided? What are the smaller topics in the text?	
Introduction	What information does the introduction provide?	
Every first sentence in a paragraph	What do I think the selection is going to be about based on the first sentence of each paragraph?	
Visuals and vocabulary	What information do the visuals add? Are there important words in bold or italics or any that are highlighted? Do I know what those words mean?	
End-of-text questions	What do the questions ask me to know? Given the questions, what do I think the reading will be about?	
Summary	What do I think the main idea will be?	

Figure 2.12: THIEVES instructional planner.

Visit **go.SolutionTree.com/literacy** *for a free reproducible version of this figure.*

For more on previewing text, including more details on and tools for using the THIEVES routine, please access the additional resources online (**go.SolutionTree.com/literacy**).

Scaffolding Strategy 6: Making Predictions

QUANTITATIVE	QUALITATIVE			
High Lexile	Levels of Meaning	Structure	Language Clarity	Knowledge Demands

In this strategy, teachers introduce students to a new text by asking them to make predictions about the reading based on their prior knowledge and the headings and subheadings, images, and words that are highlighted or in bold or italics.

Why It Matters

Taking time prior to reading the text for students to make predictions about the text is a great way to increase reading comprehension; doing so primes students' prior knowledge as well as engages them in anticipating what the text may be about (Duke, 2004; Marinaccio, 2012; Taboada & Guthrie, 2006). Engaging students in making predictions about the text provides opportunities for them to:

- Think critically about the text
- Practice using text evidence to justify their thinking
- Anticipate the characters' actions and the plot events (literary texts)
- Attend to text features such as headings, terms in bold or italics, or illustrations to enhance understanding (informational texts)
- Identify the purpose for reading the text
- Make connections to their prior knowledge, including school-home connections
- Engage in meaningful reading for authentic purposes (such as to obtain information they want or need to know)

What to Consider Before Implementing

The level of support students will need to make effective predictions will vary, especially between literary and informational texts. Literary texts follow a story sequence and pattern that is familiar to students; they contain elements like characters, setting, and plot, which students have had experience with from an early age through books and television programming. Most students have come to expect characters to experience some sort of problem and for there to be some resolution to the problem in the text, although this may be less well known among your developing readers.

In contrast, informational text is less familiar to most elementary students, so it will take more facilitation in the beginning for students to successfully leverage text features, such as headings, subheadings, captions, diagrams, and so on, to assist their predictions (Duke, 2000). For example, the way in which we might engage in informational text is less linear. You might start by referring to the index and then finding the pages that are relevant to the topic you are reading about, or you might jump from the text to a diagram to a caption as you proceed through an informational text. Furthermore, the images in an informational text serve a variety of purposes (Norman, 2010).

- **Ornamentation:** To be visually appealing
- **Representation:** To represent the written text in a visual manner
- **Organization:** To classify information (such as in a timeline)
- **Interpretation:** To use a visual to depict an abstract idea in a more concrete way
- **Extension:** To provide additional information that's not in the written text

In a literary text, however, the images are primarily representational. Given these differences between literary and informational text, when you ask students to make predictions, you will need to more heavily facilitate as students develop their skills in navigating informational texts.

> **TEACHER TIP**
>
> The following are a few suggestions for picture books that are prime material for introducing the concept of making predictions.
> - *Betcha!* by Stuart J. Murphy
> - *Big Tracks, Little Tracks: Following Animal Prints* by Millicent E. Selsam
> - *What Do You Do With a Tail Like This?* by Steve Jenkins and Robin Page

Beyond considering the type of text and its features, the prompts you use to encourage students in making predictions about the text by leveraging their prior knowledge and the text itself can be very helpful in supporting comprehension. Some example prediction prompts include the following:

- Knowing this is a narrative text, what might you be able to predict about the sequencing of the text?
- Based on the title of the text, what do you expect to read about?
- In scanning the text, what can you predict about what might happen? Be sure to provide evidence to support your prediction.
- How might the character solve the problem?

- In looking at the headings, illustrations, and captions, what do you expect the text to be about?
- What do you already know about [topic] that you might expect to read about in the text?
- What details or clues did you use to make your prediction?
- Using the images in the text, what do you expect you may learn from the text?

How to Implement the Strategy

If your students have little to no experience making predictions, you can introduce the strategy of making predictions most easily by using an interesting, thought-provoking image. For example, say students are reading a picture book and encounter an image of a rabbit, seen from behind, facing a dark wall of shrubs. There is a small opening in the shrubbery wall that reveals bright light beyond, illuminating a path in front of the rabbit. This image can lead to a great opportunity to have students practice making predictions. You can ask a variety of questions and have them justify their thinking, relying on the image and their prior knowledge.

- What is on the other side of the wall of shrubs?
- What do you think the rabbit is thinking? Why?
- Do you think the rabbit will go through the opening?
- What would make you consider going through the opening?
- What might be the source of the light coming through the shrubs?

> **TEACHER TIP**
>
> Using an image to introduce the process of making predictions has the additional benefit of reducing linguistic load for MLLs. By using a picture, you lessen the language demands of the task and invite comprehensible use of the practice. This will allow you to support all students' development of the related skills prior to practicing them with text.

Once students understand what making a prediction means, note the evidence they give to support their predictions to verify or revise later. Or, for classes who have been exposed to making predictions in the past, you may find using a prediction chart (such as the one in figure 2.13, page 46) helpful to track their predictions. Record students' responses in the first two columns prior to reading and in the third column during reading as students reflect on their predictions. To model what this might look like, I've partially filled in a prediction chart using the well-known story of "The Three Little Pigs."

Our Predictions	Why We Think That	Was our prediction verified? Do we need to revise it?
The wolf will destroy the house made of straw.	The image on page 5	Yes. It says in the text on page 6 that the wolf blew down the house made of straw.
The wolf is the villain.	Other stories like "Little Red Riding Hood" and "Peter and the Wolf"	Yes. The wolf wants to eat the three little pigs and tries to destroy their homes to get to them.
The parents will kick the pigs out of the house.	The image on page 2	No. On page 3, it says the three pigs wanted to seek new adventures, but the parents didn't kick them out.

Figure 2.13: Prediction chart example.

How to Practice the Strategy

Select an informational or literary text you'll be reading in class and fill in the prediction chart (figure 2.14), anticipating what your students would likely say. Be sure to note in the second column what details in the text or what prior knowledge may contribute to students making that prediction, particularly any misconceptions they may have.

Our Predictions	Why We Think That	Was our prediction verified? Do we need to revise it?

Figure 2.14: Prediction chart template and exercise.
*Visit **go.SolutionTree.com/literacy** for a free reproducible version of this figure.*

For more on making predictions about text, including picture examples, please access the additional resources online (**go.SolutionTree.com/literacy**).

Scaffolding Strategy 7: Reading Text With Audio Assistance

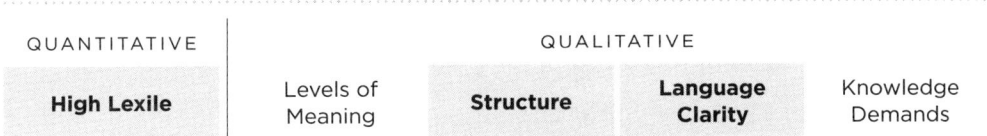

In this strategy, readers who could benefit from multiple exposures to a text listen to the audio version while following along with the text before reading it, which can be a great way to front-load and scaffold the text to increase access and comprehension.

Why It Matters

For students who are still developing their decoding abilities, providing them with the opportunity to listen to the text first fosters their comprehension of a text that otherwise might have been too difficult for them to understand through reading alone. Research shows that strong readers have comparable comprehension levels when listening to or reading a text, but for developing readers, listening to a text removes the decoding barrier and allows for comprehension to flow (Diakidoy, Stylianou, Karefillidou, & Papageorgiou, 2005; Kintsch & Kozminsky, 1977; Sticht, Beck, Hauke, Kleiman, & James, 1974). So, for grade-level readers, listening to or reading a text has little to no effect on their comprehension, but for developing readers, listening to the text can be a great strategy for leveling the playing field. Additionally, while the evidence base is small at this time, there is potential for audio-assisted reading to lead to incidental gains in vocabulary in developing readers and MLLs (Clinton-Lisell, 2023).

What to Consider Before Implementing

When training developing readers in audio-assisted reading, you will want to encourage them to not only listen to the text but also "read" the text as the audio progresses. Not only will this approach keep them more engaged, motivated, and focused on the text (Kirchhoff & Mision, 2022), but it also has the potential to help them identify new words that they can add to their reading vocabularies over time through multiple exposures (Hoskisson & Krohm, 1974). Furthermore, evidence shows that "reading" along with the audio can lead to greater improvements in reading rate and comprehension beyond the audio-assisted text (Chang & Millett, 2015; Esteves & Whitten, 2011).

If the text didn't come with an audio version, don't let that stop you from considering this strategy. You can record the text on your cell phone using a voice recorder, search the internet for the audio, or use your local library card to check out the e-audiobook of the text. You can also ask fellow staff members or faculty to record themselves reading the text. This can bring some excitement to the text as students listen and realize that the reader is their principal, librarian, and so on. One of my favorite resources for high-quality audiobooks for popular children's books is Storyline Online (https://storylineonline.net). It has famous actors as the readers, like Meryl Streep, Betty White, and Sean Astin. And don't forget that most basal reading series these days have an audio version of the text in the digital tools that come with the program.

How to Implement the Strategy

For this tech-enriched strategy, you will need the following: (1) an audio-playing device, such as an iPad, Chromebook, or similar tool; (2) headphones, if possible, to minimize distractions for other students; (3) the audio file, such as a CD or a MP3 or WAV file; and (4) a printed or digital copy of the text for each reader. As the students listen to the audio, they should be following along with the text, keeping their eyes on the words being read. I particularly like to encourage finger tracking when students engage in audio-assisted reading, as it helps them keep their focus on the text and provides a level of accountability.

Students can listen to the entire text in one sitting, or you can take opportunities to break up the text into five-to-ten-minute chunks and incorporate small-group discussion about what they have read. This will foster additional opportunities for text-based academic talk and allow you to monitor their understanding and clarify any key misunderstandings they may have developed. Figure 2.15 lists some sample questions you may consider asking.

Question Categories	Sample Questions
Main idea	• What is the main idea in this text? • What is the most important part of [paragraph or section]?
Key details	• What key details support the main idea of the text? • What do you predict will happen next? • How are [two characters] alike or different? • Describe the literary elements in the story [such as characters, setting, or sequence].
Vocabulary	• What does [word] mean? Let's use the text around it to try to figure it out. • Let's look at the word [vocabulary word]. Let's use the affix and root to try to determine the word's meaning.
Text structure	• What text structure does the author use? • How are the text features used to provide more information than the text alone?
Author's point of view and purpose	• Why does the author . . . ? • Why would the author want to draw attention to that detail?

Figure 2.15: Sample questions for monitoring understanding.

As this is a before-reading strategy, this first "reading" of the text through audio is meant to be the initial exposure to the text, followed by subsequent readings in which students engage in truly reading the text. This first "reading" is meant to give them a basic understanding of the text's key elements, which will lower the cognitive load when they decode the text on their own in the whole- or small-group reading.

> **TEACHER TIP**
>
> To support MLLs, you can pull a small group after they listen to a portion of the text and facilitate a text-based discussion providing the language supports the students may need. This could include providing additional images, asking yes or no questions, or practicing speaking in full sentences—all related to the text. The goal is to allow them more opportunities to process their understanding and to identify areas of misunderstanding that you can alleviate through the discussion process.

How to Practice the Strategy

Choose a text that you are planning to read with your class and consider which students may benefit from an additional, audio-assisted exposure to that text due to less proficient decoding skills (such as developing readers, MLLs, or students with reading disabilities). Find or create the audio to go alongside the text. Then, use figure 2.16 to craft several questions you could use to check their initial understanding of the text during or after their initial listening.

Question Categories	Questions
Main idea	
Key details	
Vocabulary	
Text structure	
Author's point of view and purpose	
Other	

Figure 2.16: Audio-assisted reading question planner.
Visit **go.SolutionTree.com/literacy** *for a free reproducible version of this figure.*

For more on reading with audio assistance, including links to children's audiobooks, please access the additional resources online (**go.SolutionTree.com/literacy**).

Scaffolding Strategy 8: Reading Aloud to Students

QUANTITATIVE	QUALITATIVE			
High Lexile	Levels of Meaning	**Structure**	**Language Clarity**	Knowledge Demands

In this strategy, the teacher reads the text aloud with visual prompts, vocabulary cards, and quotes from the text. These instructional aids support comprehension of the read aloud and prepare students to read the text in class or in a small group.

Why It Matters

To support developing readers, reading the text aloud can improve reading comprehension. When you preview the text prior to students reading it, such as by reading a key portion or the entire text aloud, you can support students' deeper understanding of the text (Amer, 1997; Dwiana, 2023; Sajid & Kassim, 2019). This allows students to leverage their listening comprehension skills and use their newly gained background knowledge of the text when they go to read the text themselves, significantly impacting their reading comprehension. An incidental benefit of this strategy is students are more motivated to engage in the text because they experience greater success due to the preparation they have received to engage in the text (Samuels, 1987). An increase in both reading comprehension and motivation is a great benefit!

What to Consider Before Implementing

This scaffolding strategy can take more teacher preparation upfront than the others, but once you build the materials, you can reuse them the next time you use that text, making the preparation minimal in future years. If you give it a try, you will see how valuable the strategy can be and that the preparation is worth the effort.

To prepare, first, you will need to create picture cards that go with the text. These pictures generally come from the student anthology stories. You will need to copy the pages from the textbook and paste them to heavier paper, like construction paper. On the back of the picture, glue the words from the text that go along with the image. In general, seven to twelve text cards are sufficient for reading the story aloud, as they provide enough visual anchors for the students to connect to and refer to. Be sure to number the images to help you as you read the text aloud. Next, create vocabulary cards of any key vocabulary that you want to draw the students' attention to during the read aloud. Finally, write up speech bubbles from the text on a third set of cards. These, like the picture and vocabulary cards, can be done on construction paper or cardstock so they will last. The last thing you will need is a large piece of butcher paper so that you can tape the picture, vocabulary, and quote cards to present the story in sequential order.

Once you have prepared all the materials, you are ready to read the text to your class. Gather your students so that they will be able to see the text as well as easily access the butcher paper. Hand out the vocabulary and speech bubble cards randomly to students; as you read the text, have them bring up the cards and put them near the part of the text in which those words occurred. Have rolled tape ready so you can add the cards to the butcher-paper chart quickly and efficiently. As you read the text on the back of each picture card, add the card to the butcher paper in the order of the text. This will aid students' comprehension as well as afford you the opportunity to use the cards for retelling practice, if desired.

> **TEACHER TIP**
>
> As you hand out the vocabulary and speech bubble cards, be thoughtful about the language proficiency levels of your MLLs. For example, if they are new to English, you may want to include a quick sketch on the vocabulary card to help them know the word or assign them a partner to assist them. Additionally, just as you might for a developing reader, you might read the word card to them so they know what it says and can put their full attention on when they should bring the card forward in the read-aloud experience.

If you have a text that does not have pictures, you can substitute with a *listen, pause, sketch* activity. This method has students sketch images to represent the pictures in their mind about what is happening in the text as you read the text aloud. This variation is also motivating because most students enjoy drawing, but keep in mind, this is meant to be sketching, not drawing. Sketching is a quick representation of the text using simple lines and loose strokes, and it lacks the more refined details a drawing would include. Sketching is for the brain and is not expected to be aesthetically pleasing. You will want to talk to your students about what you mean by *sketching*; otherwise, you may have some students who want to engage in drawing and won't be ready to continue to listen to the text after the sketching activity wraps up.

To implement the listen, pause, sketch method, you will need a piece of paper for each student, which they will fold into equal sections for recording their sketches. I usually have students fold it into six squares, with each square representing a different pause-and-sketch moment in the text. Be sure to be explicit about when they should sketch and when they should listen. Pencils should be down when you are reading until you ask students to sketch what they are "seeing" in their minds. In the end, students will have a storyboard of the text produced from their sketches.

How to Implement the Strategy

To execute this strategy, use the steps in figure 2.17 as a reference while you prepare and deliver the read aloud.

Step 1: **Text Selection**	Select a text with images that you want your students to read.
Step 2: **Text or Image Cards**	Copy the text and images. Cut them out and paste them on heavy paper, like construction paper, with the image on one side and the text on the other. Number the image and text cards in order of the sequence of the text.
Step 3: **Vocabulary Cards**	Identify key vocabulary that you want to draw your students' attention to. Write those words on strips of heavy cardstock or construction paper in large print so students can easily read them.
Step 4: **Speech Bubble Cards**	In a text with dialogue, select key quotes and write them on heavy paper in the shape of a speech bubble. If the text doesn't have dialogue, you can skip the speech bubbles or replace them with key phrases from the text.
Step 5: **Text Display**	Grab a long piece of butcher paper (approximately four to six feet) to attach the cards to, and prepare enough rolled tape to secure each of the image, vocabulary, and speech bubble cards to the butcher paper. Using a clipboard or whiteboard works great for storing the rolled tape.
Step 6: **Text Reading**	Gather students near the blank butcher-paper chart. Hand out the vocabulary and speech bubble cards to individual students. Start reading the text on the back of the image cards, following the sequence of the story. Add the image cards to the butcher paper as you read. While you read aloud, students should come up to the butcher paper and add their vocabulary and speech bubble cards when they hear you use those words or phrases.
Step 7: **Remaining Cards**	When you are finished reading, if students have any vocabulary or speech bubble cards that they didn't add to the butcher paper, work with students to determine where those cards belong, and then have them add the cards to the butcher paper.

Figure 2.17: Teacher read aloud with picture, vocabulary, and speech bubble cards.

Following the reading, there are additional activities you can do to extend the use of the materials. For example, for students who need to develop their oral language skills, such as MLLs, you can engage them in a retelling of the story. They can use the picture cards as cues. You can also add additional vocabulary cards that they may need to the butcher paper. Additionally, you can have students create a written summary of the text (using the visuals and word cards as anchors) or complete a story map (if using narrative text) to practice identifying the setting, characters, and plot. As you can see, there are numerous ways to leverage the materials for additional use and benefit.

How to Practice the Strategy

To initially prepare, gather the following materials.

- Several sheets of construction paper or cardstock
- Marker for writing words
- Scissors
- Four to six feet of butcher paper
- Glue or glue stick

Then, read the text and identify the vocabulary words and quotes or key phrases that you will include on the vocabulary and speech bubble cards. You can record those in figure 2.18 or transcribe them directly on paper strips.

Vocabulary Words	
Quotes or Key Phrases	

Figure 2.18: Reading text aloud planner.

Visit **go.SolutionTree.com/literacy** *for a free reproducible version of this figure.*

For more on reading aloud to students, including additional planning for read-aloud experiences, please access the additional resources online (**go.SolutionTree.com/literacy**).

Scaffolding Strategy 9: Discussing Text Structure

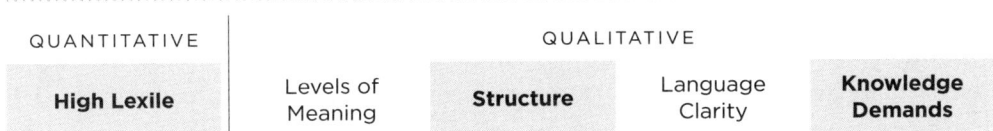

In this strategy, students learn to identify text structure elements such as setting, characters, sequence of events, and the like for narratives, and compare or contrast, sequence, or cause and effect for expository texts. This can effectively support developing readers in accessing the text more successfully.

Why It Matters

The organization of a text can undermine developing readers' ability to comprehend a text, especially expository text, but you can ameliorate this by explicitly teaching students about text structure and how to leverage a text's structure to enhance their understanding of the text (Hebert, Bohaty, Nelson, & Brown, 2016). Furthermore, text structure can impact the students' ability to accurately perceive the interaction between informational units within a text, such as events, facts, or setting (Bogaerds-Hazenberg, Evers-Vermeul, & van den Bergh, 2021). Thus, supporting students in understanding a text's structure, whether a narrative or expository text, can lessen the perceived complexity of the text; it can even be an advantage for the reader who knows how to leverage their knowledge of text structure (Arfé et al., 2018). Best of all, once students learn about text structure, they can independently transfer that knowledge to new texts, so taking the time to teach text structure has long-term benefits (Williams, 2005). Knowing that students will have increased opportunities to engage in expository text as they advance through the grades and that this foundation will serve as the vehicle for building their knowledge and making sense of the content contained in such texts, it is essential that we help students navigate a text's structure effectively.

What to Consider Before Implementing

First, there is a significant difference in the instructional time and level of complexity required to navigate text structure in different types of text. Narrative texts, in general, are much simpler for teaching students about story structure due to students having more exposure to such texts from a young age and the consistency of the text's structure, such as having a setting, characters, plot, conflict, and resolution (Hebert et al., 2016). Given the numerous types of text structures for navigating expository text (such as compare and contrast, sequence, problem and solution, cause and effect, description, and question and answer), the ways in which expository texts differ from narrative structure, and the fact that elementary-age students often have much less exposure to expository text in general, more time and intention will be needed to teach text structure for expository texts (Hebert et al., 2016).

Next, you can train students to navigate text structure to their advantage through a variety of techniques. From identifying the type of text (such as narrative or expository) to pinpointing signal words or using graphic organizers, you can scaffold student understanding while building their ability to identify the text's structure. In figure 2.19, you will find examples of *signal words*—words or phrases that indicate to the reader the type of text structure being used.

TEACHER TIP

When teaching MLLs about possible signal words that can cue them to identifying the text structure, you may need to take time in advance to front-load key terms that they may be unfamiliar with. The language used in signal words is likely challenging to students developing English proficiency, so being intentional about teaching the language of various text structures will be helpful.

Description	Compare and Contrast	Sequence
• for example • is like • such as • looks like • feels like • location words (for example, next to, below, on top of)	• both • different • however • similar to • unlike • in contrast to • on the other hand	• first, second, third, and so on • next • then • finally • after
Problem and Solution	**Cause and Effect**	**Question and Answer**
• problem • solution • solve • another way to solve • dilemma	• because • due to • as a result • since • for this reason	• how • what • why • where • who • one answer is • the question is

Figure 2.19: Example signal words by expository text structure.

In figure 2.20, you will find example graphic organizers associated with each type of text structure that you can use with students to scaffold their comprehension of that type of text.

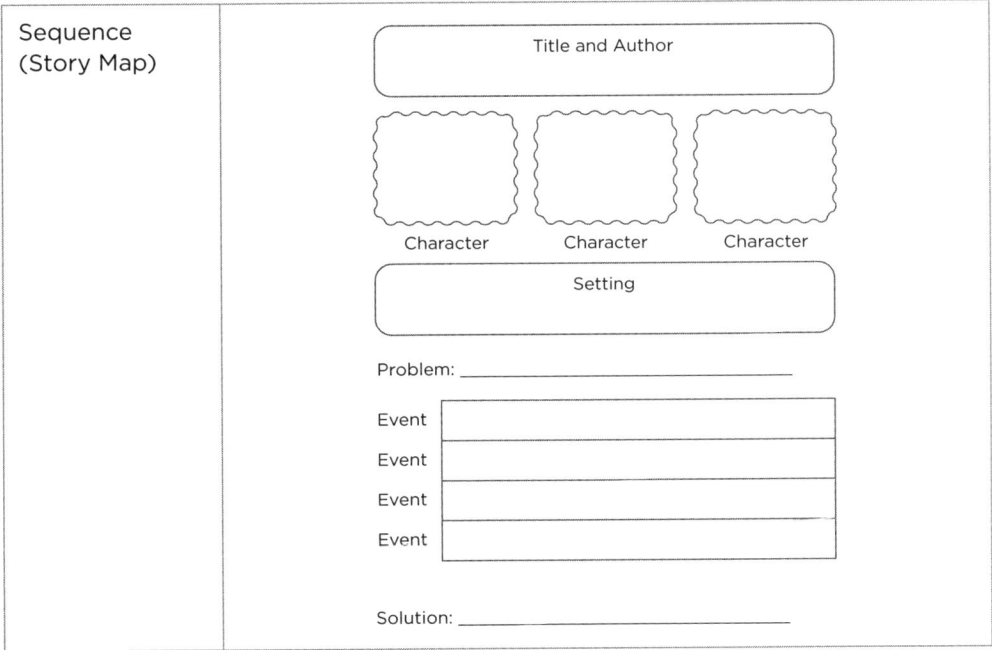

Figure 2.20: Graphic organizers by text structure.

continued →

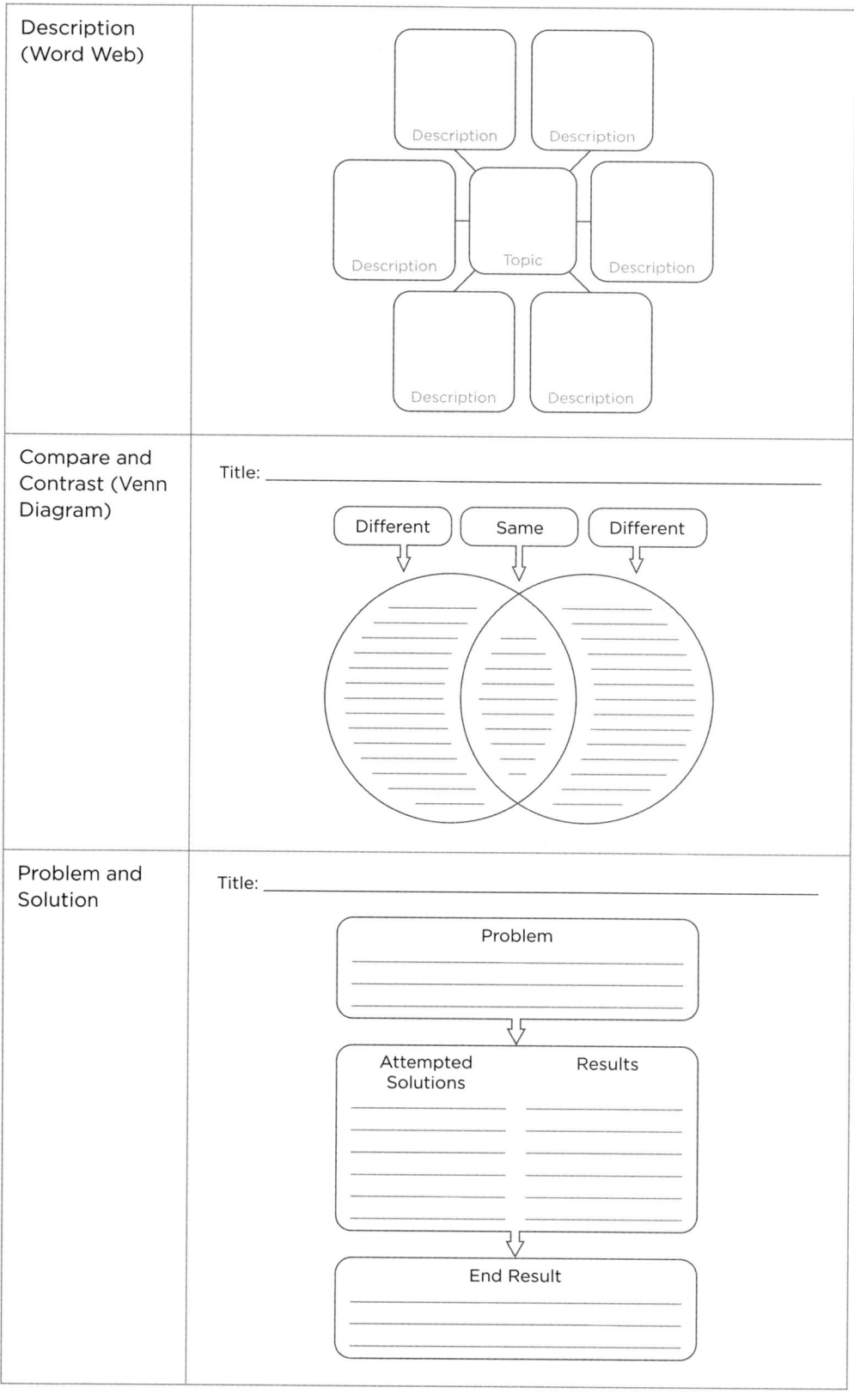

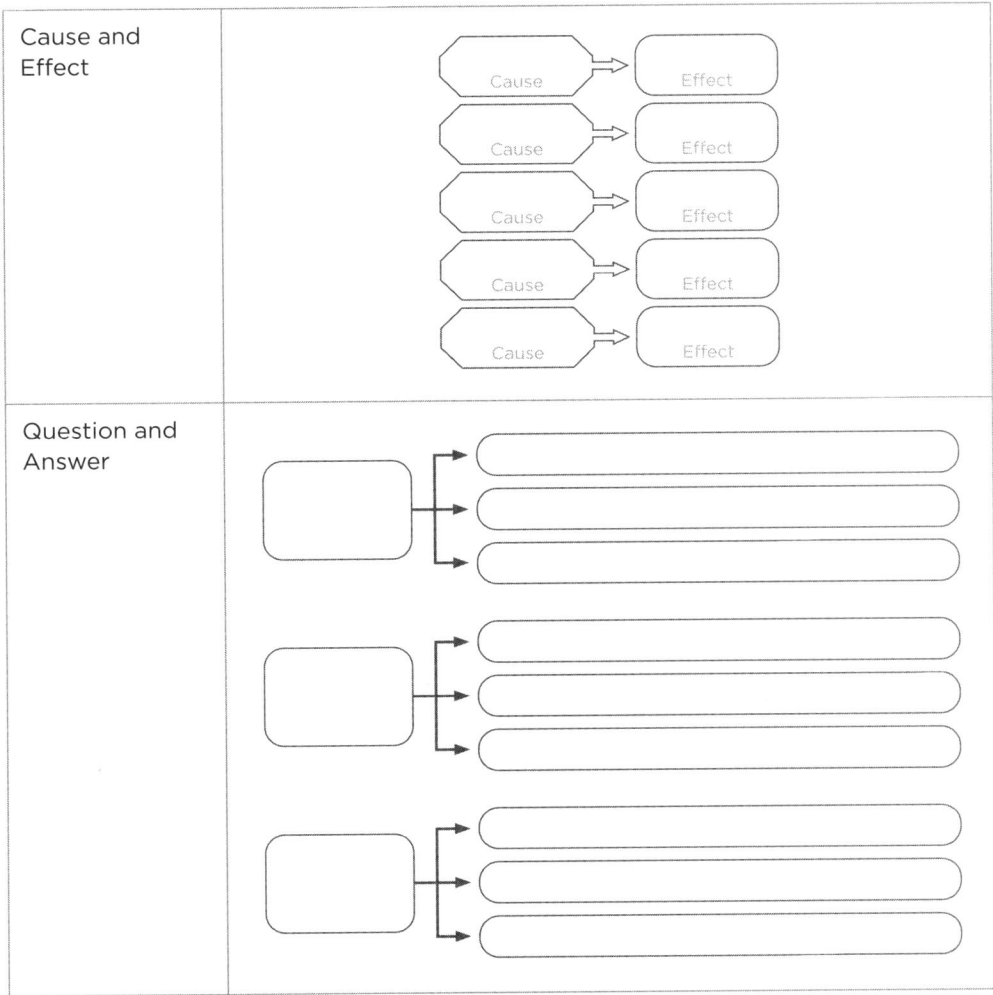

*Visit **go.SolutionTree.com/literacy** for a free reproducible version of this figure.*

To introduce the concept of text structures, education researchers Julia V. Roehling, Michael Hebert, J. Ron Nelson, and Janet J. Bohaty (2017) suggest that rather than launching it without reading materials to minimize cognitive demand, introduce it through a text structure discussion instead. For example, to introduce students to the text structure of *description*, you could ask them to describe the classroom, playground, or the school for someone who has never been there before. This would allow the students to generate descriptive details, and then you can point out how those details could create a descriptive text that portrays the chosen school setting. Then, you can move them on to mentor texts that exemplify a descriptive text structure to make the connection between the text structure discussion and the text structure used in a text.

Finally, note that attending to text structure continues throughout the text-reading process, not just before reading. For ongoing scaffolding supports during the reading, you may also want them to look for signal words, fill in the text structure graphic organizer, or make inferences about the text based on its structure as they read along.

How to Implement the Strategy

Let's use one of my favorite picture books, *Alexander and the Terrible, Horrible, No Good, Very Bad Day* by Judith Viorst (1972), to explore using text structure before reading to support reading comprehension. In case you are unfamiliar with this story, it is a narrative text that uses a sequential narrative structure organized in a cause-and-effect orientation. For example, the first page of the text describes how Alexander woke up with gum in his hair, tripped on his skateboard getting out of bed, and dropped his sweater in the sink while the faucet was on (causes), and these occurrences make him feel like it is going to be a bad day (effect). The following is an example of how a teacher might introduce the text structure before reading a text.

Teacher: *Today, we are going to be reading the story* Alexander and the Terrible, Horrible, No Good, Very Bad Day. *Our purpose for reading this text is to practice recognizing the cause-and-effect text structure. To do so, we will use a graphic organizer to record the cause-and-effect opportunities in the text and note any signal words that help us know that.*

[Hands out graphic organizer.]

Teacher: *What do we already know about cause and effect? Think to yourself.* [Waits thirty seconds.] *Now, turn to your elbow partner and share your ideas. The person with the darkest shoes goes first.*

[Students talk with their elbow partners while the teacher circulates, listening to their responses.]

Teacher: *Let's have a couple students share one idea they talked about. Naomi, will you share what you discussed?*

Naomi: *We talked about how in cause and effect, the cause is what happened, and the effect is the result of that happening.*

Teacher: *Great! So, the cause is what happened, and the effect is the resulting action or consequence. Gerome, can you add an idea?*

Gerome: *Yes, my partner and I talked about how signal words like* because, consequently, *or* since *are words we might find in the story.*

Teacher: *Absolutely.* Because, consequently, *and* since *are common signal words for cause-and-effect text structure. Don't forget, we have those signal words and a few others on our anchor chart over here.*

[Teacher points to the cause-and-effect anchor chart on the wall.]

Now, let's start reading the text. As we read along, we will pause to fill in our graphic organizer to note the causes and the resulting effect. Keep your eye out for those signal words, too.

How to Practice the Strategy

To assist you in preparing to discuss a text's structure, use the planning template in figure 2.21 to consider how you will attend to the structure before students read the text.

Text Type (Circle one.)	Narrative, Expository
Text Structure (Circle one.)	Narrative Story, Description, Compare and Contrast, Problem and Solution, Cause and Effect, Sequence, Question and Answer
Signal Words in Text	**Page or Paragraph** / **Signal Word**
Graphic Organizer (Circle one.)	Story Map, Word Web, Venn Diagram, Two-Column Chart
Page Number and Location of Content for Graphic Organizer	**Page or Paragraph** / **Related Content**

Figure 2.21: Text structure planning template.

Visit **go.SolutionTree.com/literacy** *for a free reproducible version of this figure.*

For more on discussing text structure, including graphic organizer templates, please access the additional resources online (**go.SolutionTree.com/literacy**).

Scaffolding Strategy 10: Using Text Sets to Build Knowledge

QUANTITATIVE	QUALITATIVE			
High Lexile	Levels of Meaning	Structure	Language Clarity	Knowledge Demands

In this strategy, teachers use text sets to activate students' intertextual connections and build their general and discipline-specific knowledge (Lupo, Strong, Lewis, Walpole, & McKenna, 2018). A *text set* is a collection of texts (such as articles, passages, or videos) that has been intentionally curated to explore a theme or topic in depth.

Why It Matters

When exploring a more complex concept or a topic in which students have little to no background knowledge, compiling a set of texts can be immensely helpful in easing the burden for developing readers. In fact, there are several key benefits of using text sets, including the following (Cervetti & Barber, 2009; Everett & Moyer, 2009; Lintner, 2010; Lupo et al., 2018; Scales & Tracy, 2017).

- Provides repeated exposure to key vocabulary and essential concepts
- Builds background knowledge (the number-one predictor of comprehension)
- Increases reading volume
- Incorporates complex texts through a scaffolded approach
- Increases student access to nonfiction
- Promotes deeper learning of content

This strategy is particularly useful in building background in content areas like science and social studies. You can incorporate written texts, like articles or textbook passages, with less traditional "texts" like video or audio clips, works of art, and so forth. Using a text set allows for a collection of related "texts" to work in conjunction to provide a strong foundation for accessing more complex texts on the topic, but with the basic knowledge to be able to comprehend the more challenging material (Lupo, Berry, Thacker, Sawyer, & Merritt, 2020).

What to Consider Before Implementing

As usual, the first step in considering implementing a text set is to establish your purpose for reading aligned to your content standards. Do you want to build their background knowledge and vocabulary for a complex topic or text that they will be studying? Do you want to facilitate authentic writing and research? Do you want to explore a current event? Once you have identified your purpose, then the next step is to determine whether a text set would be useful to scaffold the desired learning. To help make this determination, you can ask yourself a few key questions.

- How foreign or abstract are the concepts in the text to your students?
- Is the central text to be read set in a historical period that they are unfamiliar with and could benefit from reading about prior to reading the text?
- Does the text take place in an environment that is relatively unknown to them (like a subway setting for students in a rural community)?
- Is the language of the text rich with unknown vocabulary?

> **TEACHER TIP**
>
> There may be topics or concepts presented in your classroom that most students might be familiar with but your MLLs may not be. In that case, you can consider building text sets for small-group or English language development instruction time that can help develop the vocabulary and background knowledge that may be useful for the upcoming instruction.

Figure 2.22 is a visual representation of the steps you can take when planning to use text sets.

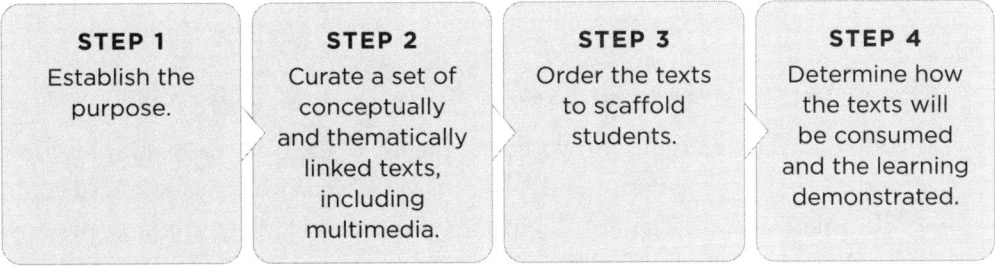

Figure 2.22: Four-step text-set-development process.

If your answers to these questions indicate that additional support may be necessary due to the demands of the topic or the text, then a text set may be appropriate. If so, you will want to take the time to curate a conceptually and thematically linked set of texts. For premade examples, see the links online (**go.SolutionTree.com/literacy**).

In curating a collection of texts, look for related texts that will build students' background knowledge and vocabulary, help them conceptualize the historical period, or otherwise assist them in understanding any challenging elements of the concept you will be teaching. Generally, a text set will incorporate text selections that are below, at, and above grade level so students can develop their reading abilities and understanding through the instructional process. Remember, your "texts" don't need to be only written texts—they can include photographs, infographics, videos, and other formats.

Once you have curated your conceptually related texts, it is time to strategically organize the texts in an order that will most effectively develop conceptual understanding. To do so, consider elements such as the complexity of the text, the vocabulary required, the content knowledge expected, and how well the text builds conceptual understanding (Garrison, 2016). For example, as you preview the texts, consider how well the key vocabulary is integrated. Is the vocabulary defined in the text, or does the text assume the reader is already familiar with the terminology? If the vocabulary is well defined, this may be a text more appropriate for early in the text set reading sequence, whereas if terms are used but little to no attention is paid to explaining those terms, then the text may be better used later in the sequence.

Now that you have selected the order of the texts, the final step is to determine your instructional plan. Which texts will the whole class read? Will students read any independently, in pairs, or in small groups? How will students show what they have learned? It may be helpful to refer to your purpose for this step, as it will be a great guide for what success looks like.

How to Implement the Strategy

Let's work through the four-step text-set-development process (refer to figure 2.22, page 61) using the topic of learning about schools around the world to exemplify how to use a text set to scaffold students in understanding complex ideas, concepts, or topics.

Step 1: Establish the Purpose

The topic—schools around the world—is aligned to the National Council for the Social Studies' (n.d.) curriculum standard *global connections*. To integrate social studies and ELA standards, the established purpose of this unit of study will be to develop second-grade students' understanding so they are able to explain, in writing, the similarities and differences among schools across the world.

Step 2: Curate a Set of Conceptually and Thematically Linked Texts, Including Multimedia

Now that the purpose is established, next, it is time to curate a collection of texts about schools around the world that will provide information for students on the similarities and differences. The text set could include books like *The Way to School* by Rosemary McCarney (480L), *School Days Around the World* by Margriet Ruurs (AD680L), *This Is the Way We Go to School* by Edith Baer (600L), a photograph collection depicting classrooms from around the world, and a YouTube video on schools around the world. The collection would highlight different ways students go to school, what classrooms look like, the resources available, and so on and would foster opportunities to compare schools from around the world.

Step 3: Order the Texts to Scaffold Students

Taking the curated resources from step 2, now is the time to put them together in an order that will scaffold the students' introduction to the key vocabulary and background knowledge they will need for the topic of study. There will be more than one way to organize them, so staying focused on your purpose and what order of instruction would make the most sense is critical. For example, you could start with the photos, as they are the least complex given the lack of language demands necessary for making sense of the "text." Students can make observations and take notes about how the classrooms in the pictures are similar to or different from their own classroom. The texts can progressively increase in complexity. You could show the video next, which provides strong visuals to complement the narrated content, and then move on to the printed texts, likely starting with the lowest Lexile text and moving to the increasingly more difficult texts. This is just one way that you could consider organizing the texts.

Another way could be looking across the texts to see what elements they address and ordering them in a fashion that builds the concept from one text to the next. For example, maybe you want to start with how students get to school, like what transportation they take—then you might want to start with *This Is the Way We Go to School*. After that, maybe you want to talk about what classrooms look like—then the photography collection and the video may be best to use next. Then you could finish with the other two books, as they reinforce the ideas of transportation and classroom designs but add additional details to the concept.

Step 4: Determine How the Texts Will Be Consumed and the Learning Demonstrated

In step 1, it was established that the students were to produce, in writing, a piece on the similarities and differences among schools around the world. So, given the broad outcome, how might you best scaffold students to be able to achieve it? You may create a table that the class can fill in as students read the texts where they can list the countries down the left-hand column and the categories of study across the top (for example, *transportation* or *classroom design*). Then, as you read the curated, ordered texts, the class can add content to the chart. Students can then turn the information from the chart into a three-to-four-sentence paragraph in which they give at least two facts about how schools are similar and one fact about how they are different.

In addition to the product, you will also want to consider how you will engage students in the texts. You might have all the students view the photos on their own during centers or stations, take notes about what they notice about the pictures, and bring their ideas to a group discussion, where their thoughts can be recorded on the class chart. You may also have them watch the video in small groups or in pairs and be ready to add ideas to the chart during whole-group instruction. Then, you may use one of the books as a teacher read aloud and the other two as teacher-supported student reads. There are a variety of ways to incorporate the texts, so just be sure you consider the amount of scaffolding, prior knowledge, and vocabulary awareness students may need to access the content, whether reading individually, in pairs, in small groups, or in a whole group.

How to Practice the Strategy

Now it's your turn to identify a topic or concept of study that your students are likely to need deeper knowledge of key concepts, vocabulary, or background knowledge to comprehend the topic at hand. Once you have identified that topic, use the resources available in your classroom, school library, and online—including those in the following section—to curate a collection using the four-step text-set-development process in figure 2.23.

Four-Step Text-Set-Development Process	
Step 1: Establish the purpose.	
Step 2: Curate a set of conceptually and thematically linked texts, including multimedia.	
Step 3: Order the texts to scaffold students.	
Step 4: Determine how the texts will be consumed and the learning demonstrated.	

Figure 2.23: Curated collection for four-step text-set-development process.
Visit **go.SolutionTree.com/literacy** *for a free reproducible version of this figure.*

For more on building knowledge using text sets, including text set examples, please access the additional resources online (**go.SolutionTree.com/literacy**).

During Reading

11. Engaging all students in active reading

12. Making connections

13. Asking and answering questions

14. Using graphic organizers

15. Chunking text

16. Engaging in structured academic discussion

17. Writing to learn

18. Summarizing texts using paragraph shrinking

Chapter Three
Scaffolding Strategies to Use During Reading

In this chapter, you will find eight during-reading scaffolding strategies to integrate into the reading of the text. It is most likely that you will use a combination of the during-reading strategies simultaneously as you engage students in reading a text. Similar to before reading, where you will always use strategy 1 (establishing a purpose for reading), you will always use strategy 11 (engaging all students in active reading) during reading, but you will also likely engage in other strategies, like strategy 13 (asking and answering questions) and strategy 14 (using graphic organizers). Your selection of which scaffolding strategies to use will vary depending on the complexity of the text and your students' ability to use the desired strategies. For example, if the text is very complex or contains novel concepts, you may want to rely on during-reading scaffolding strategies that your students know well in order to reduce the cognitive load of learning a new strategy or developing a not-yet-mastered strategy; this will allow them to focus their cognitive energy on the text rather than dividing their focus between the text and the scaffolding strategy.

As you decide on which strategies to use with a particular text, you can use the following general categories to aid your selection.

- **Interaction with the text:** To increase student engagement with and understanding of the text, you can use these strategies.
    - *Strategy 11*—Engaging all students in active reading
    - *Strategy 12*—Making connections
    - *Strategy 15*—Chunking text

- **Oral language:** To engage students in orally processing their thinking and ideas, you can use these strategies.
  - *Strategy 13*—Asking and answering questions
  - *Strategy 16*—Engaging in structured academic discussion
- **Written tasks:** To provide opportunities for students to process their thinking through writing, consider using these strategies.
  - *Strategy 14*—Using graphic organizers
  - *Strategy 17*—Writing to learn
  - *Strategy 18*—Summarizing texts using paragraph shrinking

Scaffolding Strategy 11: Engaging All Students in Active Reading

QUANTITATIVE	QUALITATIVE		
High Lexile	Levels of Meaning	**Structure**	**Language Clarity**	Knowledge Demands

In this strategy, teachers use active reading techniques and engage 50–100 percent of students in reading aloud at any given point in instruction, maximizing student participation in reading the text. Methods like *popcorn reading* or *round robin reading*—in which only one student actively reads at a time while the other students passively read—are no longer options. When using active reading engagement techniques like cloze reading, choral reading, echo reading, partner reading, duet reading, and whisper reading, every student can actively read.

Why It Matters

Providing ample practice for all learners to engage in grade-level text is essential to accelerating student reading progress. Reading grade-level text provides students with access to the key vocabulary they will need to understand the current text and subsequent texts, introduces them to concepts that will be built on across the grades, and exposes them to more complex sentence structure (Fisher, Frey, & Shanahan, 2012). So, if we want to accelerate learning, we must avoid engaging students in challenging text by using techniques like reading the text to the students, relying on the strong readers in our class to read it, or using popcorn or round robin reading, which only have one student reading at a time (Grifhorst, Lessway, & Zamborowski, 2012; Johnson & Lapp, 2012). Our instructional time is precious, and we never seem to have enough of it, so we need to get as many voices reading as possible. By using popcorn or round robin reading, we end up with one student reading at a time, but by using active reading engagement techniques, we have 50–100 percent of students reading at a time!

As educators, we diligently work to ensure every student grows in their reading ability, and to accomplish this, we must give them appropriately scaffolded opportunities to engage in text that they would be unable to read on their own. Yet, this doesn't mean that you just put the students in front of the text and say, "Read." Instead, this is where you leverage assistive reading techniques (like choral reading, echo reading, and whisper reading) to play powerful roles in providing the necessary scaffolding for the student to "lift" the heavier weight—the challenging text—through the supports you put in place to ensure their success (Bessette, 2020; Kodan & Akyol, 2018).

What to Consider Before Implementing

Given the research literature (Grifhorst et al., 2012; Johnson & Lapp, 2012) on active reading engagement techniques, there are several to choose from and some basic tenets to consider in your selection process. But, before we head into these strategies, there is one consistent practice that you should use no matter the engagement strategy, and that is ensuring students' eyes are on the text and they are actively tracking the text (Ehri & Sweet, 1991; Morris, Bloodgood, Lomax, & Perney, 2003). This may include students using their fingers or the bottom end of a pencil, pen, or highlighter to point to the text as they're reading. I even had a teacher who used those green witch fingers with red fingernails that you can find around Halloween to motivate students to track the text. So, no matter what tool you use—a finger, a pen, or a witch's finger—it is all about getting the students' eyes on the text, as there is evidence that seeing and hearing the text as they track it increases their reading skills over time (Begeny, Krouse, Ross, & Mitchell, 2009; Swain, Leader-Janssen, & Conley, 2013).

Now, I can hear you saying, "But my students won't want to track or might think finger tracking is for 'babies.'" I have heard it all. The best way I have found to overcome this resistance is to explain why you are asking them to do it. I explain to students of all ages that our brains can be easily distracted, and to help increase our focus, the simple act of pointing to the text as we read it helps the brain and improves our understanding of the text. The incidental benefit is that it can also help you, as the teacher, to know which students are with you and which you might need to redirect.

All right, let's explore six active reading engagement techniques you can use in your classroom right away to increase student engagement, reading fluency, and comprehension. Figure 3.1 (page 70) contains six research-based approaches that have proven to positively impact reading: (1) cloze reading, (2) echo reading, (3) choral reading, (4) duet reading, (5) partner reading, and (6) whisper reading. Now, this is not an exhaustive list. I have purposefully curated these six, as they take little to no preparation to implement and require at least 50 percent of students to actively read at any time. There are other research-based techniques, like reader's theater and phrase-cued reading, but those take more time to both prepare and implement, and I wanted to be mindful of how little time there is for teachers to prepare. The order of the techniques presented in the table is also intentional, with the level of scaffolding the technique provides decreasing from most scaffolding (cloze reading) to least scaffolding (whisper reading).

Active Reading Engagement Technique	What It Is	When to Use It	How to Implement It
Cloze reading	In *cloze reading*, the teacher reads the text aloud while strategically selecting words to leave out to give students opportunities to chorally read the missing words when prompted (Hasbrouck, 2010).	This technique is the most scaffolded approach you can choose, from an active reading standpoint, as the teacher does most of the heavy lifting of the text. This can be a great way to introduce students to a more challenging text for the first read, then use less scaffolded engagement techniques during the second read.	There is a certain finesse to using this technique effectively. First, you don't want to leave too many words out. A general rule of thumb is to leave out a key vocabulary or concept word once every sentence or two. If you leave words out more frequently, you may negatively impact students' reading comprehension, so be careful not to overuse the strategy.
Echo reading	In *echo reading*, the teacher models fluent reading by reading a portion of the text aloud—such as a sentence, paragraph, or page—and having students echo back with similar pacing, intonation, and expression. The teacher then repeats this pattern for as long as desired.	Echo reading is an effective way to model fluent reading with students (Raddi, 2018). You can show them how good readers pause at commas and periods, group words into phrases as they read, and add expression to their voices when they see exclamation points and question marks.	When you implement echo reading, consider the length of text your students can orally read without compromising on quality. At first, reading a sentence may be a good challenge, but over time, you will want to work up to longer echo portions of text. This ensures students don't just memorize the text and repeat it back—rather, you provide just enough scaffolding that they still have to read the text.
Choral reading	In *choral reading*, two or more students—or even a whole class—read the text simultaneously (Bessette, 2020). This technique provides developing readers scaffolded support via the more proficient readers, with the teacher modeling appropriate pacing.	Choral reading can be a great way to reengage students' interest in a text if their attention is waning or if you need to scaffold them in a particularly challenging portion of the text. That said, this is not a concern in small-group settings, so you can read longer portions using choral reading in small groups, if desired.	Sustaining choral reading with twenty to thirty voices for a long period of time can be difficult. To address that challenge, limit its use to one to three paragraphs at a time or stop occasionally to ask questions, talk about specific vocabulary, or model metacognitive thinking about the text.

Duet reading	In *duet reading*, one strong reader and one developing reader are paired to read a text aloud in unison.	Duet reading is best used when the text is two to three years above the developing reader's ability (Morgan et al., 2000). As you consider which texts or portions of text might be appropriate, you will want to aim for at least half of your class to be able to read the text with little to no support.	To implement duet reading, first establish strategic partners (see page 74). It is best for students to share one text, with the stronger reader being the pointer initially and both readers following along. Switch partners every four to six weeks to keep things fresh. Be aware that, at times, the stronger reader may be a few words ahead to ensure the fluent reading of the text, but if they are too far ahead or their partner can't keep the pace, work with the pair to make the reading more effective. By being strategic about who partners with whom, the stronger reader serves as the scaffolding that the developing reader needs.
Partner reading	In *partner reading*, the teacher pairs two students using strategic partnering (see page 74). The pair takes turns reading part of the passage aloud. This may be a page, a paragraph, or even just a sentence at a time depending on the length of the text and students' stamina (Hasbrouck, 2010). Both students should have the text in front of them and should track the text as their partner reads. The stronger reader will be able to provide prompts for unknown words for the developing reader when it is their turn to read.	Partner reading is perfect for when your students need a little motivation, as it has been proven to significantly improve engagement as well as reading comprehension (Izzati, 2023; Zulianti & Hastomo, 2022). Once you establish partnerships, it is easy to incorporate them into your instructional practice. You can employ partner reading when students start to get distracted or just need a change of pace.	In general, you will instruct one reader to go first, and then the partners alternate reading. At times, you may want the stronger reader to go first and have the developing reader reread what their partner just read. This will provide additional scaffolding where it might be needed. You also may want to vary the length of the portion the pairs read. Some pairs may have a developing reader who struggles to read one to two sentences, let alone an entire paragraph or page. You can easily personalize the amount of text the pair reads to provide extra support.

Figure 3.1: Active reading engagement techniques.

continued →

Active Reading Engagement Technique	What It Is	When to Use It	How to Implement It
Whisper reading	In *whisper reading*, students read independently in a whisper. Each student has the text in front of them, and the teacher cues when the class should start reading, usually with a prompt like "One, two, three, begin!"	Whisper reading is a great alternate technique to sustained silent reading, as it gives you actual evidence that students are reading—not just moving their eyes or fingers across the page. (It is also used in the decodable text routine in table 1.3, page 12.) As you walk around listening in, you may worry that some of your developing readers are just following their neighbor by reading the words a second or two behind. Don't worry—this is a skilled student who is independently seeking additional scaffolding. They are still engaged in the text and seeing the words on the page spoken. They may not be independently reading, but they are benefiting all the same.	Observing students as they whisper-read is a great opportunity to identify common words the class is struggling with or to gather formative assessment data on students whose reading skills you'd like to understand better. To better hear students you want to listen in on, tap on their table to signal for them to read in a normal voice. Then, tap the table again when you have heard enough, and the student can go back to whisper reading. Be sure to tell your students what the tap means before you use it! Given the varying reading rates found in most classrooms, you will likely have students who complete the text before others. You will want to explain to students that you expect them to keep reading the entire time, so if they finish before you call time, then they should go back to the beginning and read it again. Now, don't wait until every student has finished, as that is probably too long. A good rule of thumb is when about 80 percent of your class has made it through the selected portion of the text, then you can call an end to the whisper reading session.

Visit go.SolutionTree.com/literacy for a free reproducible version of this figure.

Scaffolding Strategies to Use During Reading | 73

> **TEACHER TIP**
>
> When engaging students at the early development stages of English proficiency, it may be best to add a third person to the duet reading practice. In this manner, the MLL would be seated between the two more proficient partners to be able to hear the text on both sides while following along in the text and adding in where possible.

How to Implement the Strategy

Figure 3.1 (page 70) provides substantial information on how to use this scaffolding strategy, but there are a few additional ways to leverage these active reading engagement techniques. First, given that these can be used in whole- or small-group instruction, I usually have a visual cue, such as a poster (see figure 3.2), with the six active reading engagement techniques listed on it; this reminds me to use them when we are engaging in text. Then, in a small group, you can engage students in using the poster in a couple different ways. One way is for you to roll a die to select which reading technique the group will use for the next section of the text. The first technique on the poster is selected when one is rolled, the second when two is rolled, and so on. This provides some novelty and keeps it interesting for the students. Another way you can use the poster is to allow students to choose which technique they would like to use for the next section. Now, you do have to give them a time limit to decide, or you could be waiting too long—but if you tell them they have five seconds to pick the one they will use to read the next section, they are usually successful and like the autonomy of being able to choose for the group.

Note that like figure 3.1, the order in which the active reading engagement techniques are presented in figure 3.2 is intentional: It is organized by the level of scaffolding the technique provides, going from the most scaffolded to the least. So, if the text is more challenging or complex than usual, then cloze reading, echo reading, and choral reading would provide the most support, whereas duet reading, partner reading, and whisper reading may not provide the necessary scaffolding for all students to access the text.

Figure 3.2: Active reading engagement techniques poster.

Also, keep in mind that you don't want to use too many approaches over the course of one text. I recommend using only two to three per reading of the text. This will allow students' engagement to remain high without their being distracted by wondering which technique we are using. You will also want to incrementally introduce one or two techniques at a time—again, to prevent students from spending too much cognitive energy on *how* they are reading the text versus *what* they are reading.

Finally, let's talk about how to arrange student pairs using strategic partnering. *Strategic partnering* is when you use student reading data to sort your students by their current reading abilities. Most teachers will use reading fluency rates for this ordering, but really, any data you have that are reliable and allow you to order your students will work. So, let's say you have twenty-eight students in your class. You would order your students 1 through 28, in a two-column list (see figure 3.3).

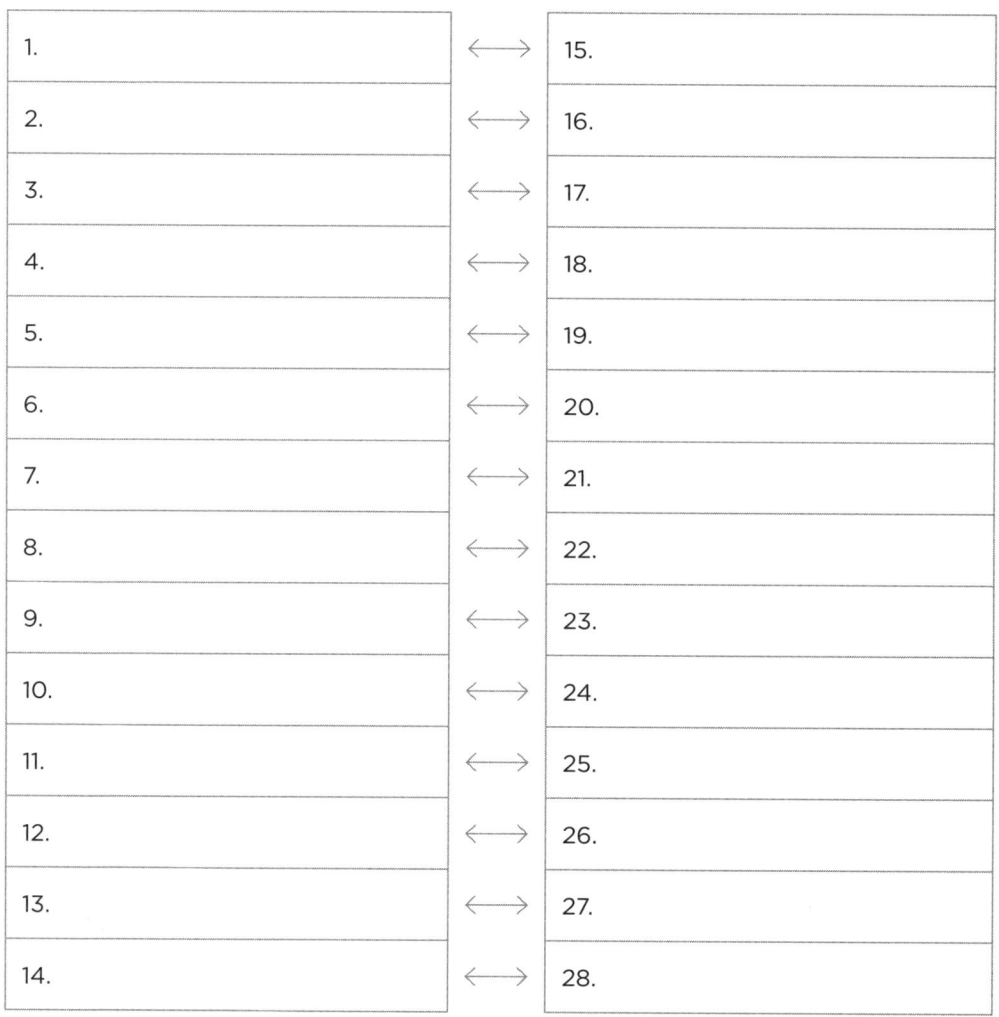

Figure 3.3: Strategic partnering.

*Visit **go.SolutionTree.com/literacy** for a free reproducible version of this figure.*

As you can see, this would match student 1 with student 15, student 2 with student 16, and so on. The benefit of strategic partnering is that it minimizes the difference in ability between the two matched students, and therefore is likely to reduce embarrassment, frustration, and confusion in both parties (Hasbrouck, 2010). Be sure to change their partnerships every four to six weeks to avoid pairs deteriorating. Also, this is not a perfect science, so if two students line up when you cut your group in half who should not be paired, then use your professional judgment and move one of the students up or down one spot. You know your students best, so do some fine-tuning to minimize problematic social dynamics.

How to Practice the Strategy

Choose a text that you will be reading soon and determine which of the six active reading engagement techniques would be best for the text. Remember, the techniques higher in figure 3.4 should provide more scaffolding, and the level of scaffolding should decrease as you move down. So, as you look at the text, if there are certain pages or passages of the text that are more challenging than others, adjust which active reading engagement techniques you select accordingly.

Text Title:		
Active Reading Engagement Technique	Circle one: Cloze Echo Choral Duet Partner Whisper	For which paragraphs or pages will you use this technique?
Active Reading Engagement Technique	Circle one: Cloze Echo Choral Duet Partner Whisper	For which paragraphs or pages will you use this technique?
Active Reading Engagement Technique	Circle one: Cloze Echo Choral Duet Partner Whisper	For which paragraphs or pages will you use this technique?

Figure 3.4: Active reading engagement techniques strategy planner.
*Visit **go.SolutionTree.com/literacy** for a free reproducible version of this figure.*

For more on active reading engagement, including models of explicit partner routines, please access the additional resources online (**go.SolutionTree.com/literacy**).

Scaffolding Strategy 12: Making Connections

QUANTITATIVE		QUALITATIVE		
High Lexile	**Levels of Meaning**	Structure	Language Clarity	**Knowledge Demands**

In this strategy, teachers have students stop in the middle of reading a text to have them consider how the text connects to their past and present experiences, helping them construct meaning. In "Making Connections Across Literature and Life," author and reading curriculum expert Kathy G. Short (1993) states that if students "make few or no connections, learning within these experiences is difficult and easily forgotten" (p. 284); however, if you can support developing readers in using what they already know to support them with the new information, you can maximize their learning.

Why It Matters

The research shows that students' reading comprehension increases when they actively construct meaning by making connections to the text, especially for developing readers (Hacker & Tenent, 2002; Kucan & Beck, 1997; Miller, 1985; National Reading Panel, 2000). These connections may stem from their personal experiences that they are bringing to bear on the text or the background knowledge they have learned from other texts on the topic. By encouraging students to make connections to the text from their background and prior experience, you can enhance the students' ability to make meaning from the text that they will more likely retain (Short, 1993).

What to Consider Before Implementing

To implement this scaffolding strategy, you can ask students questions about what they are reading and how it connects to what they already know. You can ask them about their personal experiences and how those may be similar to or different from those in the text. You can use the anticipation-reaction guide from strategy 2 (page 25) as an anchor to revisit throughout the reading of the text. The list of options goes on. The main idea is that you need to take time to pause throughout the text—or even after the reading of the text—to explicitly encourage opportunities for students to make those connections.

One research-based approach you can employ consistently across various texts is question answer relationships (QAR; Raphael, 1986). A key benefit of the QAR approach is that it provides you with a framework to design and organize your text-based questions around what will assist you in addressing both low-level questions and higher-order thinking. Both types of questions are needed to maximize comprehension. When you use this approach with some regularity, your students will start to ingrain this type of thinking into their own metacognitive practice (Raphael & Au, 2005).

> **TEACHER TIP**
>
> When you ask MLLs about their personal experiences, you will likely gain greater personal insights into their lived experiences that are likely different from your own. This is a great opportunity to learn more about your students, especially your MLLs, and to use what they share to help foster additional connections throughout the current reading and beyond. Additionally, creating this type of personal exchange can foster more productive teacher-student and student-student relationships, which can increase student interest and involvement (McElvain, 2010).

More specifically, *QAR* is an instructional approach that employs four types of questions that are divided into two categories: (1) in the text and (2) in my head. Teachers can use QAR to build reflective, metacognitive learners who can leverage their prior knowledge and experiences to make connections to text that yield increased comprehension. The four question types are shown in figure 3.5.

In the Text	In My Head
Right There The student's response is explicitly stated in the text. Example: "Who are the main characters?"	**On My Own** The student's response comes solely from the student's own prior knowledge or experience. Example: "What is a long journey you have been on that was similar to what the character in the story experienced?"
Think and Search The student's response may require them to search in the text—in more than one place—to create a list, description, sequence, or explanation. Example: "How are toads and frogs alike?"	**Author and Me** The student's response comes from making text-to-self, text-to-world, or text-to-theme connections. Example: "Why did the author include the quotation on page 4?"

Figure 3.5: Four question types of QAR.

Using these questions and explicitly teaching students how to find answers, whether those be in the text or in their head, affords them skills that they can transfer to other texts, which will aid them beyond that day's lesson. You may want to create an anchor chart in your classroom like the one in figure 3.5 to provide a reference for your students as they learn QAR.

Another way to create optimal learning conditions for making connections is to use text sets. As we established in strategy 10 (page 59), a text set is a collection of resources (books, video clips, infographics, images, and so on) that are conceptually related (Harste & Short, 1988). The benefit of using text sets for making connections is that you are directly supplying opportunities for students to make connections across texts (Cervetti et al., 2016). Using text sets gives students a prime opportunity to take what they learned from similar, previous texts and compare that knowledge with the information presented in the new text, allowing them to expand their understanding.

For example, let's say your class is studying animal habitats. As a whole class, you may read about frogs. Then, in the next text in the collection, you may read about alligators. Now, you can create opportunities through questioning that foster students' ability to compare what they learned about frogs to what they learned about alligators—how they are similar and how they are different. There is so much value in reading deeply about a topic—like habitats—and having the opportunity to make connections across texts.

How to Implement the Strategy

To clarify QAR, let's use *Where the Wild Things Are* by Maurice Sendak (1963) as an example. Figure 3.6 provides some sample questions you could use with this text to practice QAR.

Sample Question	QAR Type	Expected Student Responses
What does the word *mischief* mean?	In the Text, Think and Search	He caused trouble by making a fort, chasing the family dog, and talking inappropriately to his mom.
Why was Max sent to bed without dinner?	In the Text, Think and Search	He was impolite and unkind to his mom. He said, "I'll eat you up."
How do you think Max felt when he was sent to bed?	In My Head, On My Own	Answers will vary.
Max created an imaginary place to handle being in trouble. What do you do?	In My Head, On My Own	Answers will vary.
How did Max travel to the island?	In the Text, Right There	He went by private boat (both in the text and the pictures).
How would your reaction to the wild things be similar to or different from Max's? Why?	In My Head, Author and Me	Answers will vary.
How did Max tame the wild things?	In the Text, Right There	He stared into their yellow eyes without blinking once and scared them.

What is a *wild rumpus*? How do you know?	In the Text, Think and Search	A *wild rumpus* looks like it is dancing, yelling. Just playing around. The pictures help show what *rumpus* means.
Why do you think Max went back home?	In My Head, On My Own	Answers will vary.
If you left home like Max, what would encourage you to return? Would what worked for Max work for you?	In My Head, Author and Me	Answers will vary.

Figure 3.6: QAR sample questions for Where the Wild Things Are.

As you can see from the sample questions in figure 3.6, there are plenty of opportunities weaved throughout the text to move students from In the Text questions to the In My Head questions. If you want to use the power of making connections, you will need to create opportunities that allow students to bring their own experiences and knowledge into their reading experiences, and the In My Head QAR questions are perfect for that.

How to Practice the Strategy

Choose a text that your class will be reading soon. Use figure 3.7 to develop questions in the four QAR categories that you can use while reading that text to support students in making connections and thinking deeply about what they are reading.

Question	QAR Type	Expected Student Responses

Figure 3.7: QAR planner.

Visit ***go.SolutionTree.com/literacy*** *for a free reproducible version of this figure.*

For more on making connections, including QAR question prompts and text set examples, please access the additional resources online (**go.SolutionTree.com/literacy**).

Scaffolding Strategy 13: Asking and Answering Questions

QUANTITATIVE	QUALITATIVE			
High Lexile	Levels of Meaning	Structure	Language Clarity	Knowledge Demands

In this strategy, while reading a text, teachers and students pause during the text to ask and answer questions about what is being read. By pausing to ask and answer questions throughout the text, teachers and students model the *process* of comprehension instead of solely the *product* of comprehension. Students are actively engaged in generating questions throughout the reading.

Why It Matters

By teaching students to ask questions—also called *question generation*—about what they are reading and search for the answers to these questions, you support them in both building and monitoring their comprehension (Honig, Diamond, & Gutlohn, 2018; Oakhill, 1993; Rosenshine, Meister, & Chapman, 1996). Good readers monitor their comprehension intentionally, but developing readers often do not strategically do so (Pressley & Afflerbach, 1995), hence why you need to explicitly teach them to stop and ask questions about what they're reading. In coordination with students asking their own questions, you will also want them to answer your teacher-developed questions to further support their understanding of the text (Levin & Pressley, 1981). When used in tandem, asking and answering questions can deepen students' understanding of the text and develop their ability to self-monitor their reading. Having students ask their own questions along the way leads to students who truly monitor whether they understand what they are reading (Nolte & Singer, 1985).

> **TEACHER TIP**
>
> For students in the early phases of developing English proficiency, you may want to consider allowing them to ask and answer questions in their native language. Using assistive technology like Google Translate can be a great way to afford these students the opportunity to engage in the lesson.

What to Consider Before Implementing

In designing questions and teaching students how to generate their own questions, it is important to ensure that the questions you ask model varying levels of complexity. By using higher-order-thinking questions, you can scaffold students in increasing their reading comprehension. When engaging in a new text, you will want to start with lower complexity questions to ensure students have a basic understanding of the text before engaging in higher complexity questions. One framework you may find useful for developing questions at varying levels of complexity is Norman Webb's (2002) Depth of Knowledge (DOK) model. In Webb's DOK model, there are four DOK levels to categorize questions and learning tasks by the level of cognitive complexity they require to answer, solve, or do: (1) recall and reproduction, (2) skills and concepts, (3) strategic thinking, and (4) extended thinking. Figure 3.8 provides more information about each of the levels, a list of sample activities, and example question stems that may generally fall under that DOK level (Webb, 2002).

DOK Level of Questioning	DOK Level Description	Sample Activities	Example Question Stems
Level 1: Recall and Reproduction	Students recall, recite, or reproduce facts or use simple skills. Answers to questions involving *who*, *what*, *when*, and *where* require verbatim recall or simple understanding of single words or phrases.	Copy; find; define; identify; list; label	What is _____? When did _____ happen? Who was _____? How would you describe _____?
Level 2: Skills and Concepts	Students use information from the text to answer questions that require them to apply the information in novel ways, such as by describing or explaining *how* or *why*.	Summarize; infer; organize; compare; determine whether fact or opinion	How would you summarize _____? What do you notice about _____? How would you compare _____ with _____?
Level 3: Strategic Thinking	Students combine the knowledge they find in and beyond the text to provide a reasoned response, and they must justify their thinking.	Analyze characteristics of a genre; predict; generalize; select the best evidence and justify	How is _____ related to _____? What would happen if _____? What conclusions can you draw from _____? Justify your thinking.
Level 4: Extended Thinking	Students synthesize information from multiple sources, usually over time, or transfer knowledge from one source to a novel situation.	Compare multiple texts; explain how concepts across texts are related; synthesize information across multiple sources to generate new thinking	How are _____ and _____ the same? How are they different? Using the information from the three texts we read, explain your perspective about the causes of _____.

Figure 3.8: Webb's DOK levels.

Using the DOK levels as you plan for instruction and develop questions will help you ensure that you are creating learning conditions that require higher-order-thinking skills while providing adequate scaffolding support to allow each learner to deepen their understanding of the text. Also, DOK questions help foster students in using text evidence, as many of them require students to reference the text directly to explain or justify their thinking.

How to Implement the Strategy

So, you have written great questions. Now what? First, the order in which you deliver the text-based questions you have developed can be a strategic way to scaffold students in asking and answering questions. For example, DOK 1 ("right there" questions) is an easy place to start—it allows you to scaffold the text for the students as they find the answer directly in the text. Being explicit with students about where to find the answers in the text and modeling how to search the text for the answer can be strong supports, especially for students who have yet to realize that they can find the answers to the questions you pose either directly (DOK 1) or indirectly (DOK 2–4) in the text. Often, developing readers have not realized that looking back at the text can be a great tool for answering questions.

Beyond your strategic delivery of teacher-developed questions, there is the development of student-generated questions. To begin, you will want to model how to generate questions. To do so, start with questions on familiar topics or texts at DOK 1 and add a level or two at a time. By starting with topics or texts they already know, you can reduce the cognitive burden of learning how to generate questions while trying to understand a new text. Encourage students to focus their questions on the big ideas or important concepts of the text and to pose their questions with key words like *explain*, *how*, or *why*. For added support, you can provide them with key terms (for example, *analyze*, *describe*, *compare*) and question stems (for example, "Who was . . .?" or "Give me an example of . . .") that they can reference as they learn to write their own questions. In the beginning, students may need to work in small groups or with partners to generate questions. This will allow them to benefit from the assets that their peers bring to the process. Over time, you can transition students to generating questions from texts not previously read.

To scaffold students in generating their own questions, it may be helpful to use a graphic organizer as a question generation template. Figure 3.9 shows one example of such a template, using the fable "The Tortoise and the Hare." The key terms and question stems in the template are provided merely as examples of ways to get students thinking, and you can change or remove them at any time to provide scaffolded support. Here's how to use the template. First, students read a predetermined portion of the text and stop to generate questions to help them monitor their understanding of the text. Then, they write their question in the My Question box and develop the possible answer in the My Initial Answer box. Next, they ask their question of a peer or two and record those responses in the Peer Answers box. Finally, they compare their answer to their peers' responses and make any changes to their final answer in the My Final Answer box. By using a template like this, you can add a layer of scaffolded support as students learn to generate their own text-based questions while monitoring their comprehension of the ideas in the text.

My Question, My Final Answer

Key Terms

Identify	Explain	Make	Compare
List	Summarize	Use	Contrast

Question Stems

What did . . . ?	How would you solve . . . ?
Find the . . .	What is similar and different about . . . ?
Give an example of . . .	What caused _____ to act that way?
Describe what . . .	When did . . . ?

My Question	My Initial Answer	Peer Answers	My Final Answer
Who are the main characters? Describe how the tortoise and the hare are different.	The tortoise and the hare. The tortoise is slow, and the hare is fast.	Tortoise Hare The tortoise is wise. The hare is confident.	The main characters are the tortoise and the hare. The tortoise is slow and wise, while the hare is fast and confident.

Figure 3.9: My question, my final answer example.

How to Practice the Strategy

Select a text that you will be using with your class soon and craft questions at varying DOK levels, recording your questions in figure 3.10 (page 84). Consider developing three to four questions at each DOK level to scaffold the text through questions that guide students' understanding of important elements or ideas. See the descriptions of Webb's DOK levels in figure 3.8 (page 81) and the resources online (**go.SolutionTree.com/literacy**) to support you as you write questions.

Note that if the text you are using already has questions developed by the publisher, you can evaluate those to determine their DOK level and create any additional questions that may be necessary to ensure a variety of DOK levels are present.

Page and Paragraph	Question	DOK Level

Figure 3.10: DOK question planner.
Visit **go.SolutionTree.com/literacy** *for a free reproducible version of this figure.*

For more on asking and answering questions, including additional DOK question stem examples, please access the additional resources online (**go.SolutionTree.com/literacy**).

Scaffolding Strategy 14: Using Graphic Organizers

QUANTITATIVE		QUALITATIVE		
High Lexile	Levels of Meaning	Structure	Language Clarity	Knowledge Demands

In this strategy, teachers use graphic organizers to foster deeper student understanding of the text. Graphic organizers are visual and spatial thinking tools that help students organize information and ideas in a way that aids their understanding. Generally, graphic organizers use lines, arrows, or a spatial arrangement to provide structure and denote conceptual relationships (Darch & Eaves, 1986). Common graphic organizers used to support text comprehension include concept maps, story maps, Venn diagrams, and T-charts.

> **TEACHER TIP**
>
> Using a visual support like a graphic organizer adds structure for MLLs, as it supplements the instruction with a nonlinguistic representation that aids the textual relationships the graphic organizer facilitates. Graphic organizers reduce the cognitive demand for students having to learn content and acquire language simultaneously by providing them with the scaffolding they need to process, reflect on, and integrate information effectively (Miranda, 2011).

Why It Matters

The National Reading Panel (2000) finds that using graphic organizers increases the amount students remember about what they read. The greatest benefit of using graphic organizers to aid students' text comprehension comes from the opportunity that the visual tool provides for students to relate their prior knowledge to the new information being presented (Ausubel, 1963; Kim, Vaughn, Wanzek, & Wei, 2004; Wittrock, 1992). Additionally, graphic organizers help focus students on the most important details to be curated from the text by driving their attention to the key words and concepts and the relationships between them (Kansızoğlu, 2017). Especially in the case of developing readers, graphic organizers provide the necessary scaffolding to process information, reflect on it, and integrate it into their schema in meaningful ways. Graphic organizers are useful not only in literary texts but also in content-area reading like science and social studies.

What to Consider Before Implementing

It is unlikely that you have never used a graphic organizer before, but you may still benefit from knowing how to introduce and use them more effectively. So, first, whenever you initially introduce a new graphic organizer to your students, you need to explicitly explain the purpose of the tool and how to use it, especially for your developing readers. Developing readers are not likely to be able to make educated assumptions about how to use the graphic organizer to aid them in their reading and processing of the text without an explicit teaching model. Therefore, it is best to explicitly model how to extract information from the text and record those details on the organizer.

In subsequent uses of the graphic organizer, you can fade the amount of modeling you provide and gradually release more of the responsibility to the students. As you fade your support, you may want to consider allowing students to work in pairs or triads to practice completing the graphic organizer prior to independent practice. The rationale for doing this is twofold: (1) It allows students to verbally process their thinking with others, which is likely to improve their understanding, and (2) it builds their own capacity over time to use the tool successfully and independently in the future.

Beyond effective modeling and practice using the graphic organizer, it is critical to select the graphic organizer that is best suited for the task at hand. Think about what the purpose of reading the text is in the first place. For example, let's say you want students to compare the physical features, habitat, and diet of frogs and toads—then using a graphic organizer that visually supports those similarities and differences, like a Venn diagram, is an appropriate choice. Also, be sure not to stop at just filling in the graphic organizer and sorting the information into the appropriate boxes or sections. The power in the graphic organizer is in exploring the relationships present in the information noted. In the case of the frog and toad example, you would then want to ask students to talk about the similarities and differences using the notes they have taken. This is an essential step in using graphic organizers to maximize learning. Figure 3.11 provides a brief list of common graphic organizers and their primary uses. See strategy 9 (page 53) for several more examples.

Graphic Organizer	Graphic Representation	Primary Use
Venn diagram	Two overlapping circles labeled Item 1, Items 1 and 2, Item 2	Comparing and contrasting the similarities and differences of two concepts or ideas
Concept map	Main Item in center with six Sub Items connected around it	Sorting and classifying concepts or ideas into categories
Frayer model	Word in center with four surrounding boxes: Definition, Characteristics, Examples, Nonexamples	Exploring the examples and nonexamples of vocabulary terms and the connections between terms
Timeline	Horizontal line with boxes above and below connected by arrows	Breaking down steps or events into a sequence and identifying how the events are interconnected

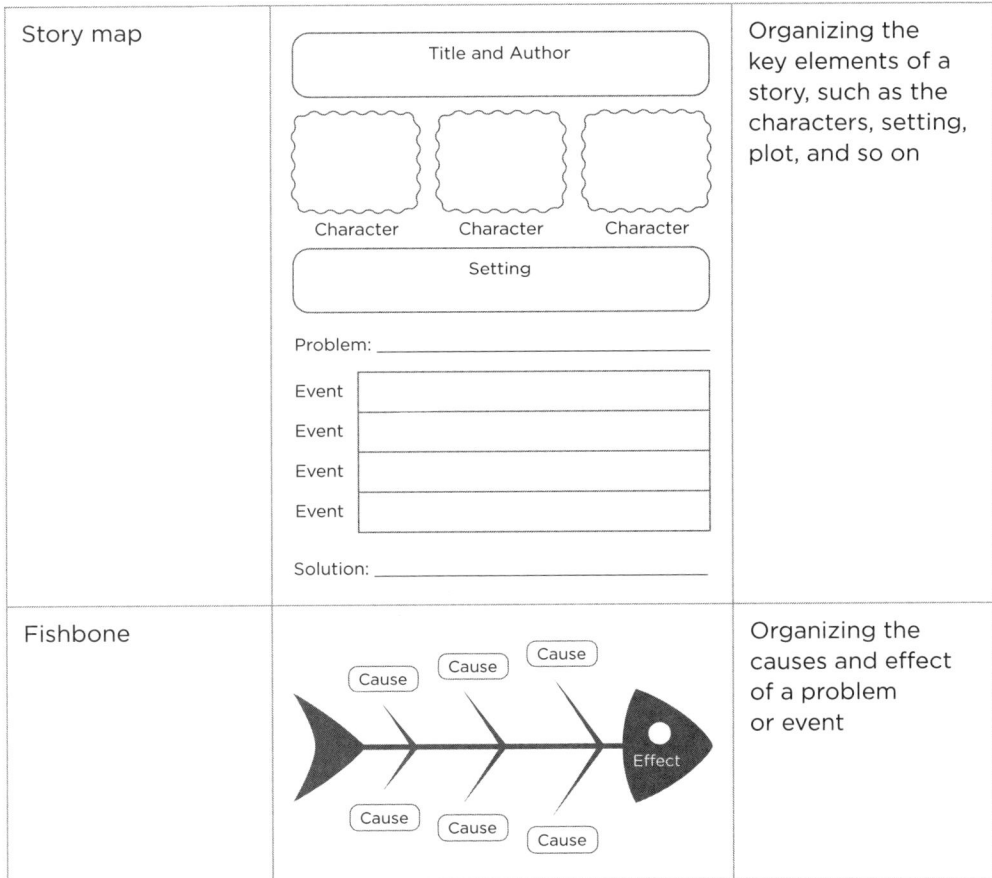

Figure 3.11: Common graphic organizers and their primary uses.

How to Implement the Strategy

To incorporate graphic organizers into your during-reading instruction, here are some key questions you can ask.

- What are your learning intentions and success criteria, as driven by your standards?
- Which graphic organizer will best support students in achieving the success criteria?
- What level of support will your students need to complete the graphic organizer?
- How will you engage students in using the information they collected?
- How will you ask students to reflect on their achievement of the lesson's success criteria?

To assist you in considering these questions, you can use figure 3.12 (page 88) as a planning and implementation tool for designing and delivering the instruction.

Instructional Order	Planning and Implementation Steps
Before Reading *Graphic Organizer Options* ☐ Venn diagram ☐ Concept map ☐ Frayer model ☐ Timeline ☐ Story map ☐ Fishbone ☐ Problem and solution ☐ T-chart ☐ Question and answer ☐ Other: _____	**Identify your instructional objective, driven by your standards,** for reading the text (for example, identify the potential causes of the Industrial Revolution; identify key details about the physical characteristics of the pink river dolphin).
	Select a graphic organizer that scaffolds students' achievement of the instructional objective (for example, Venn diagram for comparison; fishbone for cause and effect) and create a draft version of the completed graphic organizer.
	Determine how students will process their learning using the graphic organizer after the reading (for example, create a twenty-word summary of key details; debate which cause was more influential).
	Identify how you will have students reflect on how well they met the success criteria for the lesson.
During Reading	**Communicate the learning intentions and success criteria** for the lesson.
	Introduce the graphic organizer and explain its purpose for supporting the students in achieving the success criteria.
	If the graphic organizer is new to students, **explicitly model how to extract the information** from the text to complete the organizer. If the students are familiar with the graphic organizer, **provide pause points for them to fill it in during the reading.** Be sure to consider whether collaboration with peer(s) may be necessary for additional support or increased student engagement.
After Reading	**Engage students in extended discussion or writing** to process the information from their graphic organizer. **Ask students to reflect** on how well they met the success criteria of the lesson (for example, score themselves on a scale of 1 to 4, with 4 being "I can teach it to someone else" and 1 being "I am confused").

Figure 3.12: Graphic organizer planning and implementation tool.

How to Practice the Strategy

Use the planning template in figure 3.13 to prepare an upcoming lesson in which a graphic organizer would be helpful in scaffolding student understanding of the chosen text.

Instructional Order	Planning and Implementation Steps	Your Notes
Before Reading *Graphic Organizer Options* ☐ Venn diagram ☐ Concept map ☐ Frayer model ☐ Timeline ☐ Story map ☐ Fishbone ☐ Problem and solution ☐ T-chart ☐ Question and answer ☐ Other: _____	**Identify your instructional objective, driven by your standards,** for reading the text (for example, identify the potential causes of the Industrial Revolution; identify key details about the physical characteristics of the pink river dolphin).	
	Select a graphic organizer that scaffolds students' achievement of the instructional objective (for example, Venn diagram for comparison; fishbone for cause and effect) and create a draft version of the completed graphic organizer.	
	Determine how students will process their learning using the graphic organizer after the reading (for example, create a twenty-word summary of key details; debate which cause was more influential).	
	Identify how you will have students reflect on how well they met the success criteria for the lesson.	
During Reading	**Communicate the learning intentions and success criteria** for the lesson.	
	Introduce the graphic organizer and explain its purpose for supporting the students in achieving the success criteria.	
	If the graphic organizer is new to students, **explicitly model how to extract the information** from the text to complete the organizer. If the students are familiar with the graphic organizer, **provide pause points for them to fill it in during the reading.** Be sure to consider whether collaboration with peer(s) may be necessary for additional support or increased student engagement.	
After Reading	**Engage students in extended discussion or writing** to process the information from their graphic organizer.	
	Ask students to reflect on how well they met the success criteria of the lesson (for example, score themselves on a scale of 1 to 4, with 4 being "I can teach it to someone else" and 1 being "I am confused").	

Figure 3.13: Graphic organizer planning template.
*Visit **go.SolutionTree.com/literacy** for a free reproducible version of this figure.*

For more on graphic organizers, including additional, customizable templates, please access the additional resources online (**go.SolutionTree.com/literacy**).

Scaffolding Strategy 15: Chunking Text

QUANTITATIVE		QUALITATIVE		
High Lexile	**Levels of Meaning**	Structure	**Language Clarity**	**Knowledge Demands**

In this strategy, teachers intentionally break up text into more manageable pieces to increase its comprehensibility, especially for developing readers. The chunking may break up a longer piece into smaller sections or even a particularly difficult passage at the word, phrase, sentence, or paragraph level.

Why It Matters

To assist developing readers with texts that are more complex or challenging or lengthier than the student may be able to handle, you can chunk a text to make it more manageable and increase their reading comprehension (Casteel, 1988, 1990; Smith & Jones, 1992). This can also foster students' persistence and motivation with a text that they may be having a hard time reading (Fisher et al., 2012).

The scaffolding strategy of chunking text is particularly valuable for grade-level, challenging text, as such text is more likely to use more advanced sentence structure with independent and dependent clauses, pronoun referents, and synonym substitutions, which increase the complexity of the text (Casteel, 1988). You can also use chunking to provide on-demand comprehension support when students are having difficulty understanding a particular phrase, sentence, or paragraph. In this case, you can pause the reading when you notice students are not understanding, help them go back to the previously read section, and guide them in breaking down the paragraph or sentence into smaller chunks, such as by asking questions about the words and phrases in those selections to help them parse the complex sentence or paragraph.

> **TEACHER TIP**
>
> Deconstructing sentences ameliorates a variety of potential barriers to MLLs' understanding. For example, chunking the text eases vocabulary and syntax demands by having students focus on a dense portion or passage at a time, increasing their comprehension. You may find this strategy particularly useful in small-group instruction during English language development time to afford students who are developing their English proficiency more scaffolded access to grade-level material.

What to Consider Before Implementing

First and foremost, there is no one "correct" way to chunk a text. Chunking is about finding that sweet spot that provides students with just enough text that they can process and monitor their understanding prior to moving on to the next chunk of text. At each chunk of text, you need to provide a purpose prior to having students read that section. This could include giving them a question or two that you want them to answer after reading the chunk or using the information they read to fill in parts of a graphic organizer that you provide.

Another way to chunk the text is to have students use an index card to cover up text that they aren't reading yet to focus their attention on the current paragraph. Also, when students are reading on their own or in small groups, you can mark up a copied text with "stop here" signals to indicate where they should pause their reading and monitor their understanding. Example activities at the stopping points could be to record one to three key details in the margins about what they just read, underline important information that they just read, or respond to preplanned questions. As you can see, chunking has a lot of flexibility for execution while empowering students to learn to monitor their understanding of what they read with greater intention and focus.

How to Implement the Strategy

Let's take an excerpt from the book *Enemy Pie* by Derek Munson (2000) to see what chunking might look like (see figure 3.14, page 92). *Enemy Pie* is a story about a boy who turns his enemy into a friend. The Lexile is a 550L, and the book falls into the second- and third-grade Lexile band. In this example, the chunking plan is designed for a class of second graders and breaks the text up into smaller, more manageable chunks to provide opportunities for students to process their understanding of the text along the way.

How to Practice the Strategy

Choose a text that your students will be reading that is lengthier, more challenging, or more complex than what they may be able to read with success. Identify chunks of text that you can walk them through to provide the necessary scaffolding for the text and record your choices using the planner in figure 3.15 (page 93). Be sure to consider the different ways you can chunk the text depending on what is making the text challenging—for example, using index cards for focus, chunking the text into smaller parts to make it more digestible, adding stopping points with reflection questions, or adding a graphic organizer for them to complete.

For more on text chunking, including an instructional video example, please access the additional resources online (**go.SolutionTree.com/literacy**).

Chunk 1

Setting the Purpose: The teacher says, "As we read the first couple of pages, let's be thinking about why the summer wasn't perfect and why the boy doesn't like Jeremy Ross."

Page 1

It should have been a perfect summer. My dad helped me build a tree house in our backyard. My sister was at camp for three whole weeks. And I was on the best baseball team in town. It should have been a perfect summer. But it wasn't.

Page 4 (first paragraph)

It was all good until Jeremy Ross moved into the neighborhood, right next door to my best friend Stanley. I did not like Jeremy Ross. He laughed at me when he struck me out in a baseball game. He had a party on his trampoline, and I wasn't even invited. But my best friend Stanley was.

Pause and Process: The teacher asks students the following questions and has them discuss with a partner. The teacher circulates, listening in on their conversations to assess how accurate their understanding is and where they may need additional help.

Question 1: "It was supposed to be a perfect summer. Why wasn't it as perfect as he expected?"

Question 2: "Make a list of the reasons why he didn't like Jeremy Ross. Do you agree with his thinking?"

Chunk 2

Setting the Purpose: The teacher says, "As we read the next couple of pages, be ready to summarize the key information about the events that are happening."

Page 4 (second paragraph)

Jeremy Ross was the one and only person on my enemy list. I never even had an enemy list until he moved into the neighborhood. But as soon as he came along, I needed one. I hung it up in my tree house, where Jeremy Ross was not allowed to go.

Page 6

Dad understood stuff like enemies. He told me that when he was my age, he had enemies, too. But he knew of a way to get rid of them. I asked him to tell me how.

"Tell you how? I'll show you how!" he said. He pulled a really old recipe book off the kitchen shelf. Inside, there was a worn-out scrap of paper with faded writing. Dad held it up and squinted at it.

"Enemy Pie," he said, satisfied.

Pause and Process: The teacher asks students to pause after they finish reading page 6 to write a short summary with a partner of what just happened. The students must not use more than twenty words in their summaries. The teacher circulates and reviews their summaries as they write, looking for two parts: (1) the main character has made an enemy list and (2) his father is going to make him an enemy pie. A sample student summary could be: "The boy made an enemy list. His dad is going to help him get rid of his enemy with a pie." If students struggle to generate their summaries, the teacher will take them back into the text and chunk a single paragraph at a time, rereading each paragraph with the students to support deeper understanding.

Figure 3.14: Excerpt from Enemy Pie *with chunking suggestions.*

Chunk	Technique	Purpose and Learning Task
Page or Paragraph(s):	☐ Break up text into smaller chunks. ☐ Stop to pause and process using questions, summarization, a graphic organizer, and so on. ☐ Use an index card to focus their attention on a specific part of the text. ☐ Reread the paragraph, breaking down complex sentences by asking *who*, *what*, *when*, *why*, *how* questions. ☐ Other: _____.	
Page or Paragraph(s):	☐ Break up text into smaller chunks. ☐ Stop to pause and process using questions, summarization, a graphic organizer, and so on. ☐ Use an index card to focus their attention on a specific part of the text. ☐ Reread the paragraph, breaking down complex sentences by asking *who*, *what*, *when*, *why*, *how* questions. ☐ Other: _____.	
Page or Paragraph(s):	☐ Break up text into smaller chunks. ☐ Stop to pause and process using questions, summarization, a graphic organizer, and so on. ☐ Use an index card to focus their attention on a specific part of the text. ☐ Reread the paragraph, breaking down complex sentences by asking *who*, *what*, *when*, *why*, *how* questions. ☐ Other: _____.	
Page or Paragraph(s):	☐ Break up text into smaller chunks. ☐ Stop to pause and process using questions, summarization, a graphic organizer, and so on. ☐ Use an index card to focus their attention on a specific part of the text. ☐ Reread the paragraph, breaking down complex sentences by asking *who*, *what*, *when*, *why*, *how* questions. ☐ Other: _____.	

Figure 3.15: Chunking planner.

*Visit **go.SolutionTree.com/literacy** for a free reproducible version of this figure.*

Scaffolding Strategy 16: Engaging in Structured Academic Discussion

QUANTITATIVE	QUALITATIVE			
High Lexile	Levels of Meaning	Structure	Language Clarity	Knowledge Demands

In this strategy, teachers and students engage in a collaborative process in which they co-construct meaning from the text through structured text-based discussions (Wolf, Crosson, & Resnick, 2005). By providing open-ended questions that require students to describe or explain their thinking (Hiebert & Wearne, 1993), teachers facilitate student-dominated discussions about the text and encourage the use of hand gestures to foster building on each other's ideas.

Why It Matters

Engaging students in structured academic discussion scaffolds them in reading comprehension of grade-level text, with a few benefits. First, students attain the opportunity to learn by sharing their individual thoughts while benefiting from the collective reasoning of their peers, deepening their understanding and fostering their ability to provide more elaborate thoughts (Wilkinson, Murphy, & Binici, 2015). Second, it creates instructional moments where you can elicit connections to their own lives, to other texts, or to shared prior learning (Hacker & Tenent, 2002; Kucan & Beck, 1997; Miller, 1985; National Reading Panel, 2000). (See strategy 12, page 76, for more details.) Third, structured academic discussion helps build knowledge, and knowledge significantly impacts comprehension (Brown et al., 1993). Finally, using *talk moves*—or hand gestures—increases student engagement, and you can use those signals to facilitate more robust discussion. By engaging students in structured academic discussion while reading grade-level text, you can create learning conditions in which students deeply process their understanding of the text and benefit from the thinking of their peers as they do so.

What to Consider Before Implementing

As you consider how to embed structured academic discussion into your reading instruction, you'll first need to decide on the questions you'll use. It is important that they be open-ended questions, like "Why do you think . . . ?" or "How do you know . . . ?" By using open-ended questions, you enable students to more deeply explore their thinking about the reading and encourage them to be metacognitive in explaining their thinking. So, if the text you are reading is like a text you read last month, you can ask questions that encourage students to think about how the text they are reading now is connected to their prior knowledge or experience.

Beyond creating open-ended questions, you will want to facilitate ways for students to build their ideas on the insights of their peers to create a conversational flow. One way to do this is to use talk moves to create productive conversations. Figure 3.16 includes example talk moves you can use to build on student talk.

Talk Move	Hand Gesture	Description
Thumbs-Up Student puts their thumb up		Students use this gesture to indicate that they are ready to respond or have an idea to share.
Agreement Student makes a fist with their thumb and pinkie out, moving their hand back and forth between themself and the student talking		Students use this gesture when their idea is similar to what another student is sharing or when they agree with what another student is sharing.
Add-On Student stacks one fist on top of the other		Students use this gesture to indicate when they have something to add to what's being shared.
Disagreement Student points to their head		Students use this gesture when they disagree with what's being shared or have a different idea than the one being shared.

Figure 3.16: Talk moves for structured academic discussion.

It is best for students to use these talk moves in a whole-group setting, but they can use them in teacher-directed small groups, too. As the teacher, you will use the students' hand gestures to direct the conversation. For example, if the class is listening to a student's perspective and you want to bring in a different perspective to the conversation, you would look for someone pointing to their head, showing they disagree with the current idea being shared, to share next. Or, if you want to have a student add on to the current idea, then you would look for a student who has their fists stacked, indicating they have an idea that builds on what is currently being said. Using these hand signals can provide you with a great scaffold for facilitating productive, structured academic discussion that advances students' understanding while increasing their engagement.

For this scaffolding strategy, you will want to consider how you will foster engaging discussion about the text that provides ample opportunities for students to hold the floor for extended periods of time as well as how you will create the conditions to keep the conversation moving and encourage students to build their ideas on another's. This may end up being one of your favorite strategies, as you really get to hear what students are thinking and can leverage their thinking to extend their understanding and evoke meaningful connections.

How to Implement the Strategy

To support more students engaging in the thinking process for structured academic discussion, you can have students talk with a partner or in a small group prior to sharing their thinking with the larger group. This allows more students to participate than what is often possible in a large or whole-group setting and enables them to hear the thinking of others, refine their own thinking, and orally practice prior to speaking in front of the large group, which can help increase their willingness to share. You may be surprised at how many more students want to share or participate when you give them a practice opportunity first.

> **TEACHER TIP**
>
> To support your MLLs, it is particularly helpful to allow them time to discuss their responses in smaller groups prior to the whole group. It provides rehearsal of what they want to say as well as allows them to hear how their peers are framing their thinking, which will aid in how they may want to frame their own thinking. You can provide additional support by using sentence frames, starters, or word banks to help them develop academic language. (See strategy 24, page 132, for more details.)

To get the most power out of this strategy, it is crucial for everyone in the class to be able to hear the student speaking. To ensure this, you may want to share a microphone, teach students how to project their voice, or require students to stand up when they are sharing and face their peers. The conversation is only as powerful as what is being said, and if there are students in the class who can't hear it, then you may see behavioral issues arise or engagement decrease. You will want to do whatever you can to help students realize that what other students have to say is important—not just what you have to say. This may be novel for your students, so you may need to explicitly teach them the value in learning from their peers. They know it is valuable to listen to you, the teacher, but we need them to realize they can also learn from each other.

How to Practice the Strategy

Select a text that you will be reading with your class. Using the planner in figure 3.17, take time to develop open-ended questions and identify which talk moves you will teach your students to use as part of this scaffolding strategy. You may even want to consider creating an anchor chart as a visual reminder of the different ways students can show their thinking.

Page or Paragraph	Open-Ended Question
What hand signals might you want to use and teach your students to incorporate into structured academic discussion?	

Figure 3.17: Open-ended question planner.
*Visit **go.SolutionTree.com/literacy** for a free reproducible version of this figure.*

For more on structured academic discussion, including more examples of talk moves and open-ended question starters, please access the additional resources online (**go.SolutionTree.com/literacy**).

Scaffolding Strategy 17: Writing to Learn

QUANTITATIVE	QUALITATIVE			
High Lexile	**Levels of Meaning**	Structure	Language Clarity	**Knowledge Demands**

In this strategy, teachers engage students in brief, informal writing tasks (fewer than five minutes) that are focused on thinking about the key concepts or ideas of the reading selection to promote deeper understanding.

Why It Matters

Numerous studies show that combining writing and reading instruction enhances students' comprehension (Brandenburg, 2002; Collins & Madigan, 2010). Specifically, writing-to-learn tasks can be immensely helpful for supporting students in learning the content of texts, especially informational texts, by helping them organize and clarify their thoughts, which increases their retention of the knowledge they're building (Sedita, 2013). Education scholars Kathy J. Knipper and Timothy J. Duggan (2006) state that a short, informal writing task "engages students, extends thinking, deepens understanding, and continues the meaning-making process" (p. 462). When students are asked to write about what they are reading, it forces them to more deeply process the material (Fordham, Wellman, & Sandmann, 2002). If you want active, reflective readers, embedding brief writing-to-learn tasks can be a great strategy for developing such readers.

What to Consider Before Implementing

First, as you consider implementing writing-to-learn opportunities, please keep in mind that even though this strategy is housed in the during-reading strategies section, you can use it before, during, and after reading, as any time we can help facilitate students' processing of their understanding of a text through writing, it can be beneficial. For example, if you ask students to write what they know about a topic prior to the reading, you can then have them revisit their notes during and after the reading to add the new information they learned, edit information they may not have been as explicit about, or cross out misconceptions they may have had on the topic.

As you begin to incorporate writing-to-learn activities, it is best to keep them at five minutes or fewer. Any longer could make the reading feel disjointed from the writing task and distract from making meaning from the text as effectively. Brevity is key! For an informal formative assessment, walk around and monitor what students are writing. By scanning their writing, you will be readily able to note points of confusion and provide on-the-spot points of clarification. This will lead to students being more likely to acquire the desired information and more accurate understanding.

A simple way to incorporate writing to learn into your instruction is to use question words to drive students' written responses. In Judith C. Hochman and Natalie Wexler's (2017) book, *The Writing Revolution*, they explain how using question words can help students identify the most important information to record in a writing-to-learn activity. For example, providing students with key question words like *who*, *what*, *where*, *when*, *why*, and *how* can assist them in identifying the key details from the text. So, if your class read the opening pages to a narrative text, you might pause and insert a five-minute writing-to-learn activity that has them briefly respond to key question words to help them summarize what they know so far. Let's use the fable "The Tortoise and the Hare" as an example (see figure 3.18).

As you can see, once students have answered the key questions, then they can take those notes and craft a complete sentence, such as "In the forest, the tortoise challenges the hare to a race because the hare mocked him for being slow." By breaking up the details into smaller chunks like this, students will be more likely to be able to articulate the important information. The overarching goal is to make reading an interactive process that requires students to monitor what they are understanding to know when that understanding is breaking down. Writing to learn fosters such thinking and increases reading comprehension.

Key Questions

Who? Tortoise and hare

What? Running a race

Where? In the forest

Why? The tortoise challenges the hare because the hare mocked him for being slow.

Figure 3.18: Sample key questions for "The Tortoise and the Hare."

How to Implement the Strategy

To execute this scaffolding strategy, you can keep it simple by using a blank piece of paper or a whiteboard, or you can make it more structured by using a specific graphic organizer to help students organize their thoughts. This is up to your discretion, and your decision will likely be impacted by how challenging the ideas in the text are or whether a graphic organizer might assist students in making deeper connections, organizing their thinking, exploring the key concepts or ideas they're discovering, or seeing relationships in the text. For graphic organizers to consider, you can review strategy 14 (page 84) and keep reading for a few more that are specific to writing-to-learn tasks.

To support text-based responses, you can simply create a two-column chart (like in figure 3.19), where the left column shows the question posed and the right column offers space for students to record their response with evidence from the text to justify their thinking. To make the note-taking interactive, you can also have partners or small groups of students compare their responses to their peers' and see if they want to edit their answers based on their peer discussions.

Question	Response and Evidence
Why do you think the tortoise agreed to race the hare?	
What is the moral of this fable?	

Figure 3.19: Question and evidence two-column chart.

Learning logs are typically used for students to summarize key information, details, or concepts as they read a text. These can be a section of a notebook or even just some writing paper stapled together; whatever the format, the intention is to create a space for students to record their thinking as they read the text. You may even use a T-chart layout (like in figure 3.20), in which students record what the text says in the left column and what it makes them think in the right column. This is an effective way to have students identify key details from a text and make connections to their own experiences, other texts, or other shared experiences as they read along.

What the Text Says	What It Makes Me Think

Figure 3.20: T-chart learning log.

> **TEACHER TIP**
>
> For less proficient MLLs, allowing them to express themselves in their native language can be helpful. The goal of writing to learn can still be achieved by allowing them to use their native language for part or all of their response. With the ability to use technology to quickly translate those thoughts, too, you can still get a sense of what they are understanding.

When reading about topics that students may potentially misunderstand, such as the difference between energy and force, you can use the misconception check in figure 3.21 to monitor their understanding. To employ this misconception check, present statements, then have the students state whether they agree or disagree with each statement and explain why. It is a great formative assessment tool you can use to check students' understanding and see where you may need to spend more time clarifying their knowledge.

Statements	Agree? Disagree? Why?
An object stops moving because it runs out of force or energy. The terms *energy* and *force* mean the same thing.	

Figure 3.21: Misconception check.

How to Practice the Strategy

Select an informational text that you will be reading with your students soon. First, read the text and create writing prompts that will cause the students to reflect on what they have read and demonstrate their understanding of the key concepts in the text (using figure 3.22). Next, determine the format of your prompts (for example, question and evidence T-chart, learning log, misconception check, or graphic organizer). Finally, as you read the text with your class, pause to provide the writing-to-learn reflection points in your determined format.

Page or Paragraph	Writing-to-Learn Task

What format would best suit your writing-to-learn tasks?
- ☐ Question and evidence two-column chart
- ☐ Learning log
- ☐ Misconception check
- ☐ Graphic organizer
- ☐ Other: _____

Figure 3.22: Writing-to-learn planner.

Visit **go.SolutionTree.com/literacy** *for a free reproducible version of this figure.*

For more on writing to learn, including activity examples, please access the additional resources online (**go.SolutionTree.com/literacy**).

Scaffolding Strategy 18: Summarizing Texts Using Paragraph Shrinking

QUANTITATIVE	QUALITATIVE			
High Lexile	**Levels of Meaning**	Structure	**Language Clarity**	Knowledge Demands

In this strategy, students are taught how to summarize by identifying and generating the main ideas in a text to support their reading comprehension. As students work to summarize the key points, they describe their thinking to a peer and receive feedback on their thinking. Paragraph shrinking is a research-based practice from the IRIS Center's Peer-Assisted Learning Strategies (PALS) approach (Fuchs, Fuchs, & Burish, 2000).

Why It Matters

Supporting students in identifying the most important details in a text through a simple, consistent process that they can learn to independently use over time empowers them to be able to comprehend challenging texts. Using peers to assist students in learning to distill text into its most essential elements has been proven to be a highly effective strategy that increases not only comprehension but also engagement and motivation (Fuchs et al., 2000; Fuchs, Fuchs, Mathes, & Simmons, 1997). By using shrinking to explicitly teach students how to name the main idea, identify the important details, paraphrase those details, and then summarize them in a short sentence, a cognitively rigorous process becomes more accessible. Furthermore, this strategy has been particularly supportive for students with disabilities and students developing English proficiency, such as MLLs, due to the collaborative process, active dialogue, and routine structure (Sáenz, Fuchs, & Fuchs, 2005). Paragraph shrinking takes a complex cognitive process and breaks it down into comprehensible chunks, leading to great success.

What to Consider Before Implementing

If you are a kindergarten or first-grade teacher, it is best to use this strategy during read alouds when you can model the thinking of paragraph shrinking aloud. By the middle of first grade, the reading passages from your student anthology or other texts will be complex enough to model such thinking, too. If you are a teacher for grade 2 or higher, then you can teach this strategy explicitly to students and have them practice with a partner.

As you begin to implement paragraph shrinking in your classroom, you will want to establish partnerships, divide the text into appropriate chunks, explicitly teach the steps to the process, and support students in providing effective feedback to each other. To start, as this is a peer-assisted approach, you will need to establish student partnerships. Using strategic partners is best. (See strategy 11, page 68, for more information on how to strategically partner your students.) Within this partnership, the students take turns serving as the "coach" and the "reader." The coach provides the reader with feedback on each of their summary statements. The reader reads for a set amount of time, usually about five minutes, or a certain amount of text before the coach and reader switch roles. Generally, it is best to have the more proficient reader coach first so that they can model the feedback process for their partner. The coach provides feedback to the reader in a few ways: (1) by encouraging them to rethink the *who* or *what*, (2) by revising what they identified as the most important details, or (3) by determining whether their summary sentence is longer than the set limit of ten words. If the coach is unsure of what the main idea should be for a particular paragraph, they should consult you for help. Make sure to maintain the same partners for several sessions to allow the student to build up their skills prior to switching up the partnerships.

> **TEACHER TIP**
>
> For MLLs, it may be useful to use triads for this strategy. In a triad arrangement, there would be a coach and two readers. The readers work together to complete the paragraph shrinking, and the coach provides them with feedback. They then switch roles, with the two readers being the coaches and the coach being the reader. This provides additional scaffolding support for the developing MLL.

Once you have established your partnerships, it is time to model the strategy. As education researchers Douglas Fuchs, Lynn S. Fuchs, Patricia G. Mathes, and Deborah Simmons (1997) describe, there are three main steps to shrinking a paragraph down to its most essential main idea.

1. Name the *who* or *what* (for example, the main person, animal, or thing).
2. Tell the most important thing about what the *who* or *what* did.
3. Summarize the main idea in ten words or fewer. (Note: The *who* or *what*, no matter how many words, is considered one word when counting the length of the summary [for example, "the three little pigs" would be one word, not four].)

When you first introduce the steps, you will want to start with a less challenging text so that students can focus their cognitive energy on the process instead of also trying to make sense of the text. Before you pass out the text, be sure to mark it up by dividing the text into short sections or chunks. You may need to draw a line, add a star, have students mark with a sticky note, or use some other cue to prompt students so they know where you expect them to stop and think.

Next, explicitly model your thinking by explaining how to figure out what the main idea is, how to discriminate between essential and trivial or interesting details, and so on. You may also want to consider breaking up the steps of the process by adding one step at a time as students demonstrate competence. For example, you might just teach them how to identify the *who* or *what* of each section.

Then, once they are successful with that, teach them to identify the most important thing that the *who* or *what* did in that section. Finally, add the third step and have them practice summarizing those ideas by paraphrasing them in ten or fewer words. This may or may not be necessary depending on your class or grade level, but it is just another way to scaffold their learning.

Often, the most challenging part of teaching students paragraph shrinking is the feedback component. Students frequently want to just tell their partner the answer instead of giving them feedback to help them get there on their own. So, as you monitor students implementing the strategy, give them feedback on their coaching or share the great things you saw or heard during the lesson that you would like to see more—anything you can do to support students in delivering effective feedback. You can also model effective feedback anytime you are modeling the process with another student.

Paragraph shrinking is an explicit process that, if you take the time to establish strategic partnerships, select the texts and chunk the sections, explicitly model and practice the steps, and monitor and provide feedback on the students' feedback to their partners, can be a powerful strategy that students can use for years to come to support their comprehension of more and more complex text. Helping students find the gist of the text will yield great results!

How to Implement the Strategy

To make your use of this scaffolding strategy seamless, refer to the instructional routine in figure 3.23 to guide you through the process, time after time, until it becomes automatic. By using an instructional routine that is predictable and explicit, you reduce the cognitive demand of the process over time for both you and your students. As such, you have a greater likelihood of enhancing your impact on student learning.

Instructional Routine Steps	Example Teacher Actions	Teaching Tips
Step 1: Establish the purpose.	State the learning intentions and success criteria for the lesson and explain the *why* behind the strategy.	See strategy 1 (page 22) for more information on establishing purpose.
Step 2: Establish and engage in strategic partnerships.	Create strategic partnerships and model and practice the expected behaviors, such as how to give feedback.	See strategy 11 (page 68) for more on how to set up strategic partnerships.

Step 3: Distribute the text and sentence starters that students may refer to.	Hand out the text that you have marked with stopping points for students to stop and think.	Create an anchor chart with possible sentence starters they may want to use (like "The who of the text is . . .").
Step 4: Have readers and coaches practice paragraph shrinking.	Instruct students to find their reading partner(s). Then, have the first reader read the first designated section of the text and have the coach guide the reader through the steps of naming the *who* or *what*, the most important thing about the *who* or *what*, and the main idea in ten or fewer words. As the reader shares answers, the coach gives positive, corrective feedback. After a designated amount of time, usually five minutes, partners switch roles.	Have the stronger reader be the coach first, at least in the initial practice sessions. At times, you may want to collect students' ten-word summaries in writing, as this can be a great informal formative assessment. Share the paragraph shrinking prompt cards for the reader and coach (figures 3.24 and 3.25, page 106) as a reference for students as they learn the process.
Step 5: Circulate and monitor partners.	As partners work, circulate around the room to listen to the students as they read, discuss, and summarize the key points of the selection at hand. You can also provide feedback on their approach to achieving the desired results.	You may want to take notes on who is successful, who may need more support, and what you may want to bring up in the wrap-up.
Step 6: Wrap up and review the success criteria.	After partners finish or when time runs out, convene the whole group together. Have students share their answers. Depending on time, you may focus on a section that you noticed students seemed to struggle with (such as providing effective feedback or keeping summaries to the word limit) or behaviors that you want to reinforce with positive praise. Be sure to review the success criteria and have students reflect on how well they met it.	If possible, have the success criteria posted so students can refer to it as they review and reflect.

Figure 3.23: Paragraph shrinking instructional routine.

Figure 3.24 is a resource of prompts you can provide the reader to support them in knowing their role in the partnership.

Paragraph Shrinking: Reader

Step 1: Read the text aloud to your partner.

Step 2: Pause at the "stop and think" points. Tell your partner:

1. The *who* or *what*
   Sentence starter: "The *who* or *what* is/are . . ."
2. The most important thing about what the *who* or *what* did
   Sentence starter: "The most important thing about *who* or *what* is . . ."
3. The main idea in ten or fewer words

Step 3: Respond to your coach's feedback to improve your response.

Step 4: Repeat until it's time to switch roles.

Figure 3.24: Paragraph shrinking prompt card for the reader.
Visit **go.SolutionTree.com/literacy** *for a free reproducible version of this figure.*

Similar to figure 3.24, figure 3.25 is a prompt card you can provide the coach to remind them of the steps to follow when engaging in paragraph shrinking.

Paragraph Shrinking: Coach

Step 1: Follow along and track the text as your partner reads.

Step 2: Pause at the "stop and think" points. Ask your partner to:

1. Name the *who* or *what*
2. Tell the most important thing about what the *who* or *what* did
3. Summarize the main idea in ten or fewer words

Step 3: Provide the reader with any feedback they need to improve their response. If you aren't sure what the correct response is, ask the teacher for help.

Step 4: Repeat until it's time to switch roles.

Figure 3.25: Paragraph shrinking prompt card for the coach.
Visit **go.SolutionTree.com/literacy** *for a free reproducible version of this figure.*

How to Practice the Strategy

Now, it is your turn to try paragraph shrinking for yourself. Choose a text your class will be reading soon. Next, identify how you want to break up the text and mark the text accordingly. Then, practice the paragraph shrinking steps and record your ten-word summary.

1. Name the *who* or *what* (for example, the main person, animal, or thing).

2. Tell the most important thing about what the *who* or *what* did.

3. Summarize the main idea in ten or fewer words. (Note: The *who* or *what*, no matter how many words, is considered one word when counting the length of the summary [for example, "the three little pigs" would be one word, not four].)

For more on paragraph shrinking, including links to video demonstrations, please access the additional resources online (**go.SolutionTree.com/literacy**).

After Reading

19. Using text-dependent questions for collaborative discussion

20. Scaffolding with partially completed graphic organizers

21. Engaging in extended writing tasks

22. Providing sentence and paragraph frames

23. Summarizing

24. Discussing with sentence frames and word banks

25. Analyzing sentence structure using syntactic awareness

Chapter Four

Scaffolding Strategies to Use After Reading

In this chapter, you will find the final seven after-reading scaffolding strategies for processing a text more deeply after the initial reading. Your selection of which after-reading scaffolding strategies to use will depend on your intended outcomes related to reading the text. For example, if you want students to practice producing a written comparison of two characters in a text or across two texts, you would likely select strategy 21 (engaging in extended writing tasks) or strategy 22 (providing sentence and paragraph frames) to scaffold students in doing such an analysis. If you want to further develop your students' ability to identify the main idea and key details of a text, then using strategy 23 (summarizing) may be best. It really goes back to strategy 1 (page 22): What is your purpose? What are your success criteria? Answering those two questions will be your guide to choosing the after-reading strategy that yields the intended outcome of the learning activity.

As you select which strategies to use with a particular text, you can use these general categories to help you select the best strategy.

- **Advanced understanding:** If students need more opportunities to process the text to increase their understanding, you may want to choose the following strategy.
    - *Strategy 19*—Using text-dependent questions for collaborative discussion
- **Written tasks:** To engage students in processing their thinking and ideas in writing, you can use these strategies.
    - *Strategy 20*—Scaffolding with partially completed graphic organizers

- *Strategy 21*—Engaging in extended writing tasks
- *Strategy 22*—Providing sentence and paragraph frames
- *Strategy 23*—Summarizing

○ **Oral language:** To provide opportunities for students to orally process their thinking, you may consider using these strategies.

- *Strategy 24*—Discussing with sentence frames and word banks
- *Strategy 25*—Analyzing sentence structure using syntactic awareness

Scaffolding Strategy 19: Using Text-Dependent Questions for Collaborative Discussion

QUANTITATIVE	QUALITATIVE			
High Lexile	Levels of Meaning	Structure	Language Clarity	Knowledge Demands

In this strategy, teachers and students engage in an open-ended exchange of dialogue to discuss their thinking, understanding, learning, or appreciation of a text using questions that are based on the reading for the purpose of improving students' comprehension (Wilkinson & Nelson, 2013).

Why It Matters

The research evidence suggests that engaging students in collaborative discussions about text can increase their reading "comprehension, metacognition, critical thinking and reasoning" (Murphy, Wilkinson, Soter, Hennessey, & Alexander, 2009, p. 743). More specifically, collaborative discussions foster opportunities to more deeply process a reading selection, where students engage in productive conversations with their peers and the teacher that are dominated by student talk and facilitated with the teacher's open-ended, authentic questions (Raphael et al., 1992; Wilkinson & Nelson, 2013). By engaging in collaborative discussions, students get to examine new ideas and consider alternative ways of thinking and speaking about their understanding of the text. Peers serve as models and provide ideas that may represent different backgrounds and perspectives, yielding opportunities that can broaden a student's own thinking (Eeds & Wells, 1989; Knickerbocker & Rycik, 2006). Additionally, peer interactions mediate students' reasoning, thus allowing them to refine and deepen their understanding (Murphy et al., 2009). Engaging in meaningful, absorbing discussions with peers and the teacher can dramatically enhance comprehension.

What to Consider Before Implementing

To increase the likelihood that collaborative discussions will yield learning, there are some important factors to keep in mind. First, you need to establish a clear purpose for the discussion. For example, you could ask students to:

- Critique the text for its strengths and limitations
- Reflect on the author's approach to the text
- Make connections to other texts
- Relate ideas from the text to their personal experiences or feelings
- Gather key information from the text to use in their writing
- Prepare for a class debate

Whatever the purpose, clearly communicate it to the students so they understand the goals of the discussion.

Next, you will want to be thoughtful about how you engage students in the discussion. Collaborative discussions are more than putting students into groups and encouraging them to talk. A more intentional approach is needed because less proficient readers are less likely to engage in whole-class discussions compared to proficient readers (Hall, 2012). Using specific protocols to foster meaningful discussion that achieves the intended purpose and fosters productive interactions can help alleviate this natural tendency. You will find a few examples of structured discussion protocols in the following section that you can choose from. Your purpose and the students you serve should drive your selection of the structure that best fits the lesson's desired outcomes.

One last consideration when implementing collaborative discussions is ensuring you create a space that is open to the ideas, opinions, and interpretations of others, allowing students to collaboratively construct meaning (Almasi & Garas-York, 2009; Bridges, 1979). Discussions should be based on open-ended questions—not a single correct interpretation of the text—in order for students to arrive at new, deeper understandings of the text (Almasi, 2002).

To increase the effectiveness of such discussions, you will likely need to explicitly teach students how to listen to ensure a fruitful experience (Raphael et al., 1992). One way to explicitly teach students to listen is through the *four L's of listening*, adapted from Kate Kinsella's (2012) *four L's of productive partnering*. The four *L*'s of listening are as follows.

1. Look at the speaker's eyes.
2. Lean toward the speaker.
3. Lower your voice.
4. Listen attentively.

> **TEACHER TIP**
>
> Be mindful of how students' cultural identities might influence their listening behaviors. For example, in some Native American cultures, it is disrespectful to look someone in the eye. It is important that we consider our students and discuss how they might perceive the directive to "look at the speaker's eyes."

By teaching these four behaviors, students will have the moves to benefit from what they hear from their peers. Creating an anchor chart as you introduce the four *L*'s as an ongoing reference point would be helpful, too. This will allow you to quickly review the listening expectations and refer to them when giving students feedback or reflecting on how they did at the end of the lesson. While the four *L*'s were initially designed to promote productive partnering, they can easily be adapted to small-group discussions.

Finally, as students learn to engage in productive conversations about text, they will need to learn how to build on each other's ideas (Raphael et al., 1992). To support students in doing so, you can use collaborative discussion sentence frames. Such sentence frames give students the academic language they need to build on each other's ideas. Some example sentence frames include the following:

- I want to expand on your point about . . .
- I agree with what _____ said because . . .
- I thought about that also, and I'm wondering why . . .
- Based on the ideas from _____, _____, and _____, it seems like we all think . . .

You will want to have these sentence frames or similar language visually available for students to refer to. This could be in the form of a handout or an anchor chart, but any avenue that gives them the language they need to build on each other's ideas explicitly and intentionally will do.

How to Implement the Strategy

So, now you have a sense of the factors to consider and implement to foster productive collaborative discussions that allow students to negotiate their understanding and refine it as needed. The following are three example discussion protocols you can use.

Save the Last Word for ME

Save the Last Word for ME (Averette, n.d.) is a process intended to support students in clarifying and deepening their understanding of the text by responding to and building on each other's thinking. Students work in groups of four, with one member as the timekeeper. In preparation for the small-group discussion, ask each student to identify what they consider to be the most important idea in the text and highlight that section. In the group, one student shares the section of the text they found most important and reads it out loud to their group. The other members of the group listen to the passage and consider what the student is sharing. Afterward, the other three students each have one minute to respond to the passage that the first student shared. This might include what it makes them think about, what questions it raises for them, and so forth. The first student then shares why they selected that section and responds to or builds on the ideas that they heard from their peers. This process repeats until all members of the group have shared their selection.

Four A's

Four A's (National School Reform Faculty, 2015) is a process intended to support students in better understanding a text by asking them to consider four perspectives. It is best used with texts that allow for multiple perspectives. After finishing the reading, post the four *A* questions.

1. What *assumptions* does the author of the text hold?
2. What do you *agree* with in the text?
3. What do you want to *argue* with in the text?
4. What parts of the text would you want to *act* on?

Next, in groups of four, students refer to the text to respond to each question. It may be helpful to have students work in pairs prior to the discussion to identify responses to each question. Additionally, you could share the four *A*'s prior to the reading and encourage students to annotate while they read, using these four questions to drive their annotations. This would expedite the discussion at the end of the reading.

In each round, each group member shares their idea for responding to one of the *A* questions and cites the text (with a page number) as evidence for their thinking. Once the students have discussed the four *A*'s in their small groups, you can facilitate a whole-class discussion.

Graffiti Wall

A *graffiti wall* (Facing History and Ourselves, 2008) is an interactive approach in which students move around the room in small groups to respond to posted questions. A graffiti wall provides students the opportunity to reflect on the text and to process their thinking in a cooperative way. First, post large pieces of paper with text-dependent prompts or questions around the room. You will want enough questions to break up the class into manageable groups. The students rotate around the room, responding to each question in writing or with drawings. Over the course of five to ten minutes, as the students move from question to question, they review the previous groups' contributions and add their response based on the question and what has already been added to the paper. After students have added their responses to each chart, facilitate a whole-class discussion about those same text-dependent questions.

How to Practice the Strategy

Now, it is your turn to identify and plan how you will support your students in engaging in collaborative discussions. Use the writing space in this section to think about how you might explicitly teach them the discussion protocol you may want to use for your chosen text or how to listen and build on others' ideas. There are some additional resources in the following section you may want to consult as you plan.

For more on text-dependent questions, including additional language frames and examples of collaborative discussion protocols, please access the additional resources online (**go.SolutionTree.com/literacy**).

Scaffolding Strategy 20: Scaffolding With Partially Completed Graphic Organizers

QUANTITATIVE	QUALITATIVE			
High Lexile	Levels of Meaning	Structure	Language Clarity	Knowledge Demands

In this strategy, teachers create and partially complete a graphic organizer (such as a Venn diagram, timeline, or concept map) that represents the relationships between facts, details, and ideas from a text to support students' ability to identify the most essential content.

Why It Matters

Using partially completed graphic organizers can provide the needed scaffolding to help students focus on the most essential details from a text. For developing readers, identifying the most critical information from a text without getting lost in the minutiae can be challenging. By incorporating partially filled-in graphic organizers after reading a text, you can help your students hone their focus, more easily notice relationships, and increase their retention of new learning (Colliot & Jamet, 2019; Robinson et al., 2006). Additionally, this strategy can increase conceptual connections and the likelihood that students will be able to apply their newly learned knowledge in novel situations (Katayama & Robinson, 2000). Graphic organizers are designed to organize information hierarchically, which generally makes it easier for students to retain and retrieve new information (Bean, Singer, Sorter, & Frazee, 1986; Bransford, 1979).

> ### TEACHER TIP
> Research shows that partially completed graphic organizers can be very beneficial for MLLs. Specifically, they can help MLLs (1) prioritize what is essential to know, (2) reduce information processing demands, (3) demonstrate how to structure information, and (4) influence positive attitudes toward reading (Ellis, 2004; Mede, 2010).

Perhaps best of all, by having some of the graphic organizer filled in, you reduce the cognitive burden—especially for young, developing writers who may still be growing their fluency with letter formation and basic spelling—as well as the instructional time needed to complete the organizer. By using and scaffolding partially completed graphic organizers, you can balance both the content students collect and the learning they experience, which yields improvement. It is not solely about filling in the graphic organizer (Ponce, Mayer, López, & Loyola, 2018) but also the cognitive process that readers go through to make sense of a text and organize the key information in usable ways.

What to Consider Before Implementing

The research literature on graphic organizers suggests that providing a graphic organizer alone has minimal impact on learning; for a graphic organizer to have impact, you must explicitly teach and model its use for your students (Carnes, Lindbeck, & Griffin, 1987; Clements-Davis & Ley, 1991). So, if you are going to use this strategy, you will need to be mindful of how you will model your thought process, evoke the thinking of students as peer models, and provide guided instruction to maximize the benefit of the tool and ultimately impact comprehension and learning. Over time, you will want to reduce the amount of modeling and coaching you provide for the graphic organizer so that students can learn to be less dependent on your prompts and cues to internalize the process and thinking. Graphic organizers can be useful before, during, and after reading—it is all about how you will integrate them. For more information on using graphic organizers, see strategy 14 (page 84).

How to Implement the Strategy

To use a partially completed graphic organizer, you can follow these four steps.

1. **Choose a graphic organizer:** Select the best graphic organizer given your established purpose, intended learning outcomes, and the text.
2. **Complete the graphic organizer:** Draft a complete version of the graphic organizer containing all the desired details. Save a copy.
3. **Create the partially completed graphic organizer:** Identify what information is most important and replace that information with blanks.
4. **Explicitly guide students' completion of the graphic organizer:** After students have read the text, distribute the partially completed graphic organizer and explicitly guide students through the thinking process required to fill in the missing elements.

Now that you know the steps, let's use the familiar text "The Three Little Pigs" to model what the instructional planning steps look like in action (see figure 4.1).

Step 1: Choose a graphic organizer. Select the best graphic organizer given your established purpose, intended learning outcomes, and the text.	The intended purpose is to practice orally retelling "The Three Little Pigs" using the key elements of a story, such as the characters, setting, and plot. As such, a story map would be the most appropriate graphic organizer to support the intended learning outcome. Students will refer to the completed graphic organizer to support them in retelling the key details of the text.
Step 2: Complete the graphic organizer. Draft a complete version of the graphic organizer containing all the desired details. Save a copy.	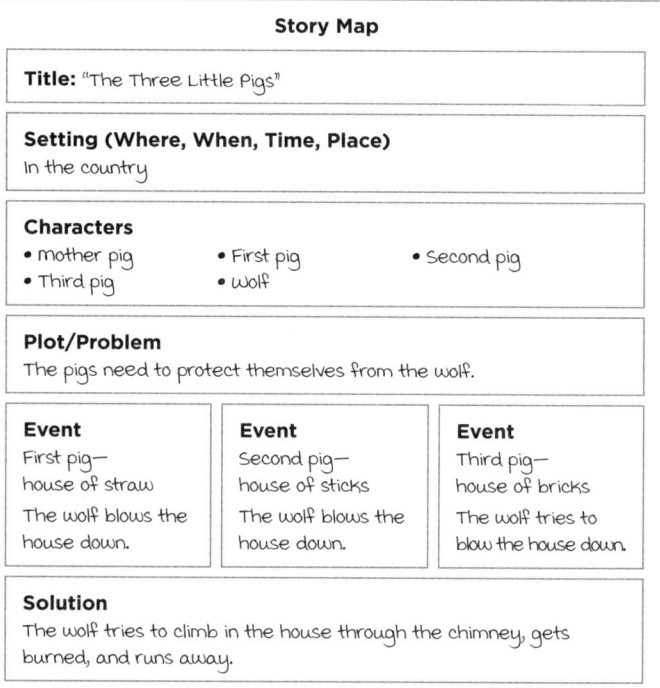

Step 3: Create the partially completed graphic organizer. Identify what information is most important and replace that information with blanks.	**Story Map** **Title:** "The Three Little Pigs" **Setting (Where, When, Time, Place)** **Characters** • mother pig • First pig • _____ • _____ • _____ **Plot/Problem** The pigs need to protect themselves from the wolf. **Event** First pig—house of _____ The wolf _____ _____. **Event** Second pig—house of _____ The wolf _____ _____. **Event** Third pig—house of _____ The wolf _____ _____. **Solution**
Step 4: Explicitly guide students' completion of the graphic organizer. After students have read the text, distribute the partially completed graphic organizer and explicitly guide students through the thinking process required to fill in the missing elements.	Walk students through each section of the graphic organizer. Have them discuss the answers and refer to where in the text it says that or where they can infer it. Model how to add the missing information to the partially filled-in graphic organizer along the way. Students may have to use different words when crafting the problem, solution, and so on, but their responses should be accurate. Provide corrective feedback as needed.

Figure 4.1: Instructional planning sequence for "The Three Little Pigs."

How to Practice the Strategy

Select a text and a graphic organizer for which using a partially filled-in graphic organizer will support students in comprehending the text more deeply. For example, if the text is structured in a compare-and-contrast form, then a Venn diagram would be appropriate; if it presents multiple events over time, then a timeline might be most helpful. (You may want to refer to strategy 14, page 84, for some of the most common tools.) Then, fill in the graphic organizer as you would expect your students to do so. Review the completed organizer and remove some of the information that you will fill in with students during instruction. Use the following space or another sheet of paper to record your draft.

_____
_____
_____
_____
_____
_____
_____

For more on graphic organizers, including customizable templates, please access the additional resources online (**go.SolutionTree.com/literacy**).

Scaffolding Strategy 21: Engaging in Extended Writing Tasks

QUANTITATIVE	QUALITATIVE			
High Lexile	Levels of Meaning	Structure	Language Clarity	Knowledge Demands

In this strategy, students engage in writing assignments that require them to reflect, revisit the text, or make connections and identify relationships within and across texts or experiences over an extended period of time.

Why It Matters

Engaging students in extended writing tasks is proven to enhance their reading comprehension, even more than answering questions or reading and studying alone, especially for students with learning disabilities or developing readers (Graham & Hebert, 2010; Hebert, Graham, Rigby-Wills, & Ganson, 2014; Hebert, Simpson, & Graham, 2013).

Perry D. Klein (1999) explains that extended writing can facilitate comprehension for four reasons:

> 1) writing fosters explicitness and structured thinking through semantic and syntactic choices,
>
> 2) it creates a permanent product that can be reviewed and transformed when contradictions arise,

3) it encourages authors to construct relationships among ideas, and

4) it may help writers to generate and revise goals for the audience based on new content and ideas. (as cited in Hebert et al., 2014, p. 44)

Given these connected benefits of using extended writing to improve comprehension, affording students opportunities to process and extend their understanding of text in writing is a useful scaffolding technique, especially for developing readers.

What to Consider Before Implementing

As you implement extended writing tasks to scaffold students' comprehension of challenging texts, here are three key elements to consider from Steve Graham and Dolores Perin's (2007) meta-analysis on using extended writing tasks.

1. Provide clear, explicit product goals that articulate to students the purpose of the extended writing task as well as the characteristics expected of the final product.

2. Use mentor texts, also known as *study of models*, to support students in generating their own writing.

3. Integrate writing in content-area learning to enhance content knowledge development, including in mathematics, science, and social studies.

> **TEACHER TIP**
>
> The three key elements for implementing extended writing tasks are even more critical for MLLs because they provide clearer expectations, give models, and expose them to meaningful, grade-level-appropriate content knowledge that is essential to accelerating their growth.

In relation to these three key elements, there are a variety of different ways you can incorporate extended writing in the classroom. Some ideas include having students:

- Summarize what they have read (see strategy 23, page 125)
- Create research reports after reading multiple texts on a topic, like the habitat, diet, and survival adaptations of local animals
- Craft a book, article, or text review
- Develop an alternate ending for the text
- Draft a new text based on a mentor text (such as on text structure or figurative language)

The overarching idea is that using extended writing tasks can encourage students to revisit the text, reflect on what they have learned, and leverage the information in novel and unique ways, such as those I described in the preceding list. With a well-defined purpose and explicit expectations for the end product, you can use extended writing tasks to effectively deepen students' understanding and build their knowledge.

How to Implement the Strategy

Let's say you are working on developing students' understanding of the cause-and-effect text structure. To do so, you choose to do an author study of Laura Numeroff using books in her *If You Give* series, such as *If You Give a Mouse a Cookie* or *If You Give a Cat a Cupcake*, as mentor texts to model cause and effect. After reading a few of her books, you might assign students to write their own "If you give . . ." statements as their extended writing assignment. As part of scaffolding them to be successful in the assignment, you might provide sentence frames like the following.

- If you give a _____ a _____, they're going to ask for _____.
- When you give them _____, they'll probably ask you for _____.

By having students engage in crafting their own stories, you enable them to dig more deeply into the semantic and syntactic choices of the author as models for their own writing. This will contribute to deepening their understanding of both the actual texts under consideration as well as the chosen text structure. After their initial drafts, you might even reread one of the texts (or read another one) and have them pay particular attention to the text structure; then, have them go back and consider how they might enhance their first drafts. Overall, by engaging the students in an extended writing task, you advantage them to a stronger understanding of the text and how it functions.

How to Practice the Strategy

Consider a reading selection you have coming up in language arts, science, social studies, or another area of study that might lend itself to an extended writing task to strengthen the students' text comprehension. Identify the writing task that you want to assign to the students and then consider what instructional supports you might provide to scaffold them in the writing assignment to extend their reading comprehension. As a reminder, examples could include using mentor texts as models, conducting research reports, writing a summary of the text, and so on. Record your extended writing task in the space provided.

For more on extended writing tasks, including additional examples, please access the additional resources online (**go.SolutionTree.com/literacy**).

Scaffolding Strategy 22: Providing Sentence and Paragraph Frames

QUANTITATIVE	QUALITATIVE			
High Lexile	Levels of Meaning	**Structure**	**Language Clarity**	Knowledge Demands

In this strategy, teachers use sentence and paragraph frames as skeletal frameworks to scaffold student oral and written language. By providing a portion of the paragraph, teachers give students a guide on how to organize and develop the ideas they want to express. A paragraph frame on students' favorite animals might look like the following.

_____ is my favorite animal. One reason I like _____ is _____.

Another reason is that _____.

There is no other animal like _____ because _____.

Why It Matters

Using sentence and paragraph frames as temporary scaffolds can be a powerful mechanism for supporting developing readers in cultivating academic language and thinking skills while increasing their comprehension (Zwiers, 2004). Through repeated practice with frames, you can:

- Strengthen students' development of strong academic sentences and paragraphs
- Provide practice using transitional phrases to model effective writing
- Encourage varied sentence structure (such as simple and complex) and text structure (such as compare and contrast or description)

Using a paragraph frame aids students in learning the structure of a paragraph (such as a topic sentence, related details, and a conclusion), generating ideas for a paragraph, and practicing writing and reading their own text (Adams, 2008). Over time, the frame can be slowly stripped away, where students do more and more of the writing to the point where they no longer need a frame, as they have internalized the elements.

> **TEACHER TIP**
>
> Sentence and paragraph frames have been found to be particularly useful for MLLs, as they serve as a mechanism for explicitly teaching writers the academic language they need to communicate, with the necessary scaffolding for building their confidence (Zwiers, 2004). Additionally, they allow MLLs to express their ideas at a more complex level than their current proficiency.

What to Consider Before Implementing

Sentence frames are designed so that students provide the missing target words or phrases to complete the sentence. So, if your class read a text on the benefits of solar energy, you might provide a sentence frame or two for them to respond to a question like "What are the benefits of solar energy?," such as:

- One benefit of solar energy is _____.
- A couple benefits of solar energy include _____ and _____.

By providing the sentence frame, you scaffold full academic responses and prime students for articulating their thoughts in writing later, with exemplars for doing so. You may also want to model using the frame for students so they can see how it works. Be sure to tell them that they can't use your example when they share their ideas with their partners or the class.

A single-paragraph frame typically has the following components.

- An introductory sentence that restates the question or topic of study
- Two or more examples that support the question or topic
- Transition words
- A conclusion sentence that sums up the paragraph

Please note that you can have more than single-paragraph frames. It is really up to you how much scaffolding and support you provide.

In general, with sentence and paragraph frames, you should consider the level of support your students need. Some students may need more support than others. So, you can consider using a sentence or paragraph frame as a support that students can choose to use, but be clear that you still expect them to write full academic sentences. If a student chooses not to use the frame but doesn't produce the level of quality you expect, then you could recommend they go back and use the frame so that they can demonstrate a stronger performance.

How to Implement the Strategy

The following is an example teacher script to show you how you might implement sentence frames in the classroom.

Teacher: *Now that we have finished reading the first section of the article, let's discuss what we have read about the benefits of solar energy. On your own, I want you to generate a list of the benefits of solar energy that we learned about in the article. Please write your list in your reading journal.*

[Students take a few minutes to review the text and write down a list of the benefits of solar energy.]

Teacher: *As I was walking around, I saw you record some great ideas in your journals about the benefits of solar energy. Now, I want you to share one or more of your ideas with your elbow partner. If the idea your partner shares is not already on your list, please add it. When you share your idea, you will use one of these two sentence frames.* [Teacher writes the options on the whiteboard: "One benefit of solar energy is _____" and "A couple benefits of solar energy include _____ and _____."] *Let's read the sentence frames together.*

[Students chorally read the two sentence frames out loud.]

Teacher: *So, if I were completing the sentence and I had written down in my journal the word* renewable, *I would tell my partner, "One benefit of solar energy is it is a renewable resource that doesn't run out." All right, your turn. Take turns stating your idea to your elbow partner using one of the sentence frames on the board.*

[Students turn and talk to their elbow partners, using the sentence frames and one or more of the ideas they noted in their journals from the text.]

Teacher: *Let's come back together and hear from a few of our classmates about their ideas. Angie, would you go first?*

Angie: *"One benefit of solar energy is it has a low carbon footprint."*

Teacher: *Put a thumb up if you also shared about solar energy having a low carbon footprint.*

[Students who also selected this idea hold up their thumbs to show they had similar thinking.]

Teacher: *Great! It looks like several of you had that idea. José, how about you? What did you share?*

José: *"A couple benefits of solar energy include it is a renewable resource, and it doesn't produce any noise."*

Teacher: *Hold your thumb up if you also chose either that it is a renewable resource or that it doesn't produce noise.*

[Students who also selected this idea hold up their thumbs to show they had similar thinking.]

Teacher: *Nice! It looks like many of you had similar ideas to José.*

Figure 4.2 is an example paragraph frame.

The Benefits of Solar Energy
by _____
Solar energy, a _____, is one of several options for meeting _____.
One benefit of solar energy is _____. Another unique benefit of using solar energy is _____. Yet, the best benefit is _____ because _____.
Considering these benefits in comparison to other types of energy, like _____, _____, and _____, solar energy has some advantages.

Figure 4.2: Solar energy paragraph frame.

Figure 4.3 shows how you could use figure 4.2 to support students in writing about the benefits of solar energy.

Instructional Process
1. **Develop the paragraph frame.** Create a paragraph frame that aligns with your established purpose for the lesson and models the type of writing you'd like to see your students be able to produce independently over time.
2. **Review the paragraph frame.** Display the paragraph frame and explain to students that you will give each of them one to fill in the missing information with the ideas they learned from the text.
3. **Read the paragraph frame.** Chorally read the paragraph frame with the class. After reading it, go back and talk about what ideas students could write in the blanks.
4. **Distribute the paragraph frame and monitor.** Hand out the paragraph frame and circulate around the room to provide positive, clarifying, and corrective feedback to students as needed.
5. **Wrap up.** Have students practice reading their paragraph frames to a partner. They may make corrections as they go as needed. Then, identify one or two paragraph frames that you want to share as exemplars. This is a great way to explicitly highlight specific traits in their writing that you would like to foster in others'.

Figure 4.3: Instructional process for using paragraph frames.

How to Practice the Strategy

Grab a text that you will be using soon and develop either sentence frames or a paragraph frame that aligns with your established purpose for that text and provides scaffolded support for students to develop academic language at the sentence or paragraph level based on the important details from the text.

For more on sentence and paragraph frames, including examples for various grade levels, please access the additional resources online (**go.SolutionTree.com/literacy**).

Scaffolding Strategy 23: Summarizing

QUANTITATIVE	QUALITATIVE			
High Lexile	Levels of Meaning	Structure	Language Clarity	Knowledge Demands

In this strategy, students engage in a reading and writing process in which they identify what is most important in what they have been reading, condense the information while keeping it accurate yet succinct, and rewrite it in their own words. Summarizing requires the student to decide what they need to include, what they can eliminate, and how to sequence the information, all while maintaining the integrity of the author's original meaning (Anderson & Hidi, 1988–1989).

Why It Matters

The mental and physical act of writing a summary is an effective way to support readers in identifying the most important ideas and details that improves both their retention of the information and their reading comprehension (Dollins, 2011; Hebert et al., 2013; Marzec-Stawiarska, 2016). This is the case for several reasons. First, by explicitly and systematically teaching students how to summarize, you make them more aware of how the text is arranged and how those ideas are related (Graham & Perin, 2007; Lehr, Osborn, & Hiebert, 2005). Summarizing requires students to identify the key information and make connections among those ideas (Armbruster, Anderson, & Ostertag, 1987). Furthermore, it positively improves their vocabulary and overall learning (Brown, Campione, & Day, 1981; Hidi & Anderson, 1986).

What to Consider Before Implementing

Through the act of summarizing, students both deepen their understanding of text and prepare for additional learning activities you may engage them in, such as essay and report writing, oral presentations, and other after-reading tasks. The complex task of creating a written summary to synthesize ideas from the text activates both reading and writing skills. Researchers Bruce Saddler, Kristie Asaro-Saddler, Mariola Moeyaert, and Julienne Cuccio-Slichko (2019) find the following in their study:

> In terms of reading, the writer must decode and comprehend a text, identify important content, and create a shortened, accurate account of the original textual source or sources approximating the original authors' key ideas, purpose, and intent in a paraphrased version that includes essential supporting details. (p. 572)

In terms of writing, however, the writer must condense the essential information from one or more texts to create a new text that is reflective of the original piece.

Considering the layers of thinking required, using summarizing as a scaffolding technique may seem unusual, but there are ways to ease students into this powerful strategy, thus reducing its cognitive demand. The three key suggestions for introducing summarizing in an accessible manner for developing readers include the following (Anderson & Hidi, 1988–1989).

1. **Use narrative texts:** Narratives are easier to summarize than informational texts, so starting with narratives will ease the learning process.

2. **Use shorter texts:** By starting with shorter text pieces, you allow students to encounter a smaller amount of information, reducing the amount of sifting necessary to find the main ideas and details. Over time, you can practice summarizing with increasingly longer texts.

3. **Use less complex texts:** Start by using texts that are less complex, like texts on topics familiar to your students; ones that use common, everyday language; or ones with text structures that are easy to follow. Just as with the length of the text, you can increase the complexity as students build their capacity.

Beyond selecting the appropriate texts, be sure to allow students to refer to the text while they are summarizing it. This frees them from having to purely use their memory, and it will result in a more complete summary. Also, be aware that young learners often lean toward pulling out the unusual ideas as opposed to the most important, so it is helpful to be explicit about what makes an idea important (for example, it supports the main idea; it is essential for understanding the text; it provides concrete facts or details that support the main idea; and so forth).

How to Implement the Strategy

For this scaffolding strategy, you will want to use a routine process each time your students engage in summarizing; this will help them be able to focus on the ideas in the text rather than the thinking process required to find those details. One specific instructional routine you can use for informational text is the WINDOW method (Saddler et al., 2019). WINDOW stands for:

- **W**rite a topic sentence
- **I**dentify important information
- **N**umber the pieces of identified information
- **D**evelop sentences
- **O**rganize sentences using transition words
- **W**rite an ending sentence

By providing this mnemonic, you enable students to internalize the process over time so they will be able to rely on it to walk themselves through summarizing text. As students learn the process, you can use example student summaries as opportunities to use the WINDOW method to evaluate if the summary contains those six components. This will provide students with explicit feedback on what those six components should include and will deepen their understanding.

> **TEACHER TIP**
>
> Using instructional routines is extra powerful for MLLs. Routines maximize instructional time by creating consistency in language and process, which improves students' understanding through repetition and practice, ultimately building automaticity while reducing cognitive load (Valencia Goodall, Gomez, & Webster, 2024).

To explicitly teach the WINDOW method, it is useful to start by creating an anchor chart with the mnemonic and defining language for ongoing reference. Additionally, as you teach students the steps, you can provide additional prompts and supports to help scaffold the process. Figure 4.4 (page 128) provides an example of the additional details or prompts you can provide for each step.

In figure 4.5 (page 129), you will find a template for using WINDOW with students in the early grades. This template has a place for drawings to help support beginning writers.

In figure 4.6 (page 130), you will find a template for using WINDOW with intermediate writers. These templates are meant to be temporary scaffolds that you can remove as students adopt the mnemonic.

WINDOW Method Step	Supporting Prompts
Write a topic sentence	• What is the main idea? • What is the text about? • Scan the titles, subtitles, visuals, and other text elements.
Identify important information	• Highlight, circle, or underline. • Reread sections to find the important details. • List key facts, reasons, or ideas.
Number the pieces of identified information	• Organize the details into an understandable order. • Add a number next to the important information to indicate the order.
Develop sentences	• Take the important information and craft sentences in your own words. • Restate the important details in your own words and combine where appropriate.
Organize sentences using transition words	• Shrink and combine sentences to make your summary more succinct. • Add transition words to connect ideas.
Write an ending sentence	• Remind the reader of the main idea. • Reiterate the most important ideas.

Source: Adapted from Asaro-Saddler, Muir-Knox, & Meredith, 2018.

Figure 4.4: Supportive prompts for the WINDOW method.

The WINDOW mnemonic is great for informational text, but it doesn't lend itself as well to narrative text structure. Therefore, you may want to have a different routine for summarizing a narrative. Valerie Ellery (2005) developed a simple routine called *Somebody Wanted But So Then* for summarizing fiction. Using the keywords of the routine, students ask themselves five questions.

1. **Somebody:** Who is the main character?
2. **Wanted:** What did the character want?
3. **But:** What was the problem?
4. **So:** How was the problem solved?
5. **Then:** How did the story end?

They then take their answers to those questions and craft summary statements. Creating an anchor chart with the keywords and the guiding questions can be a great reference for students when they are working to summarize a narrative text. Also, providing a simple graphic organizer, like the one in figure 4.7 (page 131), can offer some structure while students learn the process. For beginning writers, you can model using the graphic organizer several times before turning the writing over to the students. For intermediate

Name: ______________________ Date: ____________

Write a topic sentence		
Identify important information and **N**umber the pieces of identified information	Draw	
Develop sentences and **O**rganize sentences using transition words		
Write an ending sentence		

Figure 4.5: WINDOW template for beginning writers.

Visit ***go.SolutionTree.com/literacy*** *for a free reproducible version of this figure.*

Name: _____ Date: _____

Write a topic sentence	

Identify important information and **N**umber the pieces of identified information	
Develop sentences and **O**rganize sentences using transition words	
Write an ending sentence	

Figure 4.6: WINDOW template for intermediate writers.

Visit go.SolutionTree.com/literacy for a free reproducible version of this figure.

Name: _____	Date: _____
Title of Text: _____	

Somebody	
Wanted	
But	
So	
Then	
Summary	

Figure 4.7: Somebody Wanted But So Then template.
Visit **go.SolutionTree.com/literacy** *for a free reproducible version of this figure*

writers, you could still model a few times in whole or small group, but you can start them on writing more quickly. Over time, as students become more proficient with the strategy, especially older students, you can have them complete the graphic organizer in small groups, with a peer, or individually, with the goal to be truly independent.

How to Practice the Strategy

Choose the appropriate WINDOW template for the age of your students. Select a short, less complex text that has familiar content. Practice filling in the graphic organizer so you have a sample of what a complete product looks like. This will help you be able to facilitate a more effective first-time use of the WINDOW summarization method. As with any routine, take time in the initial uses of the mnemonic to explicitly teach what each section is for and the process for each step.

For more on summarizing, including a link to a demonstration lesson and more sample templates, please access the additional resources online (**go.SolutionTree.com/literacy**).

Scaffolding Strategy 24: Discussing With Sentence Frames and Word Banks

QUANTITATIVE		QUALITATIVE		
High Lexile	Levels of Meaning	Structure	**Language Clarity**	**Knowledge Demands**

In this strategy, teachers use *sentence frames* (fill-in-the-blank sentences) to provide linguistic structure for students to express their thinking and *word banks* (lists of text-specific words and phrases) to give students words to draw from as they discuss the text. Both support students in developing and using the academic language of the content they are studying.

Why It Matters

When engaging students in challenging texts—especially discipline-specific ones, like in science or social studies—the level of academic language and the conceptual knowledge demand are high (Fisher et al., 2012). Sentence frames and word banks can help mediate these demands and support students in developing their conceptual understanding and the language they need to express that understanding (Shimada, 2017). They provide scaffolded supports that leverage the content-specific language of the text, allowing students to practice discussing the concepts they are learning to develop the necessary academic language and to comprehend the text (Bray Donnelly & Roe, 2010). They also provide a model that supports students in producing a complete thought that incorporates academic language (Rosa Le Bron, 2020). If you want your students to acquire the content-specific language, they need to practice using it, and sentence frames and word banks promote such acquisition (Kinsella, 2005).

What to Consider Before Implementing

As you implement sentence frames and word banks into your instruction, there are a few key things to consider. First, be sure your sentence frames are open enough to allow multiple ways for students to respond using the frame. The goal is scaffolding, not mimicking. You want to leave the frame open enough that there are a variety of ways students can accurately respond. Second, allow students the choice to use the frame or not. Some students may be able to produce more advanced oral language than the frame would allow, and we do not want to hamper students in expressing themselves in a more advanced way. The frame is there to be a support, not a confinement. Finally, be aware of when it is time to remove the sentence frame or word bank. When you notice students demonstrating that they can speak precisely using the academic language of the text independently, it is time to withdraw the support. As with any scaffolding strategy, it is meant to be temporary.

Additionally, sentence frames and word banks are intended to elevate students' oral and written production. Being intentional with the design of your sentence frames and word banks serves two main purposes: (1) to help students better comprehend the content and its associated academic language and (2) to develop their command of the English language to advance their oral and written production. One way to identify areas of opportunity is to review students' writing samples to identify the types of language structures they could use more support in developing. Students are unlikely to write language that they cannot already say, so this is a great way to identify their needs. For example, while reviewing a collection of work from young writers, you might notice that they overuse the sentence starter "I like." If you want to try to encourage more variety in their sentence writing, then having them practice a sentence frame such as "I like _____ and _____" would be helpful. Or, if you want to increase the variety of language in their sentences, using a word bank for phrases that also mean "I like"—such as "I prefer," "I adore," or "I am partial to"—would expand their vocabularies.

Finally, using an instructional routine when implementing sentence frames can increase the effectiveness of the practice. Education scholars Whitney Bray Donnelly and Christopher J. Roe (2010) suggest the following routine: "Listen to me say the sentence; now you say it with me; now say it to me; finally, say it to your partner. After guiding students through the process several times, have them practice with each other" (p. 135). Whatever routine you choose, be sure that it is consistently and explicitly delivered each time.

How to Implement the Strategy

To effectively incorporate sentence frames and word banks into your after-reading instruction, you will need to engage in a series of easy steps to best prepare and deliver. First, read through the text prior to classroom instruction and identify the key vocabulary students would need to know to understand the concepts (Bray Donnelly & Roe, 2010). Consider which terms you may need to front-load prior to reading the text due to their criticality to understanding the text. (See strategy 4, page 32, for more information on front-loading vocabulary.)

Next, develop the sentence frames or word banks that you want to provide to scaffold student talk about the text while developing their use of the reading's academic language. Be mindful of what linguistic structure you intend to serve. For example, do you want to more fully develop your students' ability to make more complex sentences by incorporating conjunctions? If so, then developing sentence frames that require the use of *or*, *but*, or *and* would be valuable. Or perhaps you've been reading a science text that compares plant and animal cells. Providing sentence frames or word banks with the language of comparing and contrasting would be useful. A few example frames might include the following.

- Plant cells and animal cells are similar because _____.
- Another way they are alike is _____.
- One way that plant and animal cells differ is plant cells _____, while animal cells _____.

After front-loading key vocabulary and completing the initial reading of the text, introduce the sentence frame or word bank and model how to use it. You will want to bring students' attention to the grammatical features that you are infusing into instruction here, too. So, going back to the conjunctions example, you would explain that students can create more interesting and complex sentences by using words like *or*, *but*, or *and* to craft their sentences. In this way, you move students beyond purely copying the language to thinking about how it is structured and building their understanding for future use (Barko-Alva & Chang-Bacon, 2023).

TEACHER TIP

If you have students with varying levels of English proficiency, you may want to consider providing differentiated frames. By doing so, you acknowledge the students' current language levels and afford them great opportunities to meaningfully and successfully engage in the discussion. So, for example, if you ask students to compare, you might have three different sentence frames they can choose from.

1. **For emerging MLLs:** Plant cells and animal cells have _____.
2. **For developing MLLs:** Plant cells and animal cells are both _____, but plant cells are _____, and animal cells are _____.
3. **For expanding MLLs:** The main difference between plant cells and animal cells is plant cells are _____, while animal cells are _____.

Finally, use the instructional routine in figure 4.8 to engage students in using the sentence frame or word bank.

Step 1: Read the text and select the key vocabulary needed to understand the concepts. Identify which words to front-load prior to reading the text. To align with effective practice, limit your selection to two to three words per day.
Step 2: Craft sentence frame(s) or word banks to scaffold the academic language connected to the topic at hand. Consider differentiating the frames for varying levels of English proficiency, if needed.
Step 3: Front-load the most essential vocabulary prior to reading the text.
Step 4: Engage students in reading the text.
Step 5: Introduce the sentence frame or word bank and model how to use it. Discuss and point out the grammatical structures related to the type of language being produced (for example, comparison language or combining sentences with *or*, *but*, or *and* to make compound sentences).
Step 6: Use an instructional routine to execute the sentence frame or word bank activity. Provide syntactic and content guidance as needed.

Figure 4.8: Instructional design and delivery for using sentence frames or word banks.

How to Practice the Strategy

Choose a text that has some challenging concepts and vocabulary for your students. Use the instructional planning template in figure 4.9 to craft sentence frames or word banks for an after-reading discussion that encourages students to discuss the important concepts while incorporating the key vocabulary.

Step 1: Read the text and select the key vocabulary needed to understand the concepts, recording them in the right column. Identify which of those words to front-load prior to reading the text and underline them.	
Step 2: Identify which syntactic structures are related to the type of language structure desired (for example, comparison or the use of conjunctions). Consider the needs of your students based on writing samples.	
Step 3: Craft sentence frames or word banks to scaffold the academic language connected to the topic at hand. Consider differentiating the frames for varying levels of English proficiency, if needed.	

Figure 4.9: Instructional planning template for sentence frames and word banks.

For more on sentence frames and word banks, including tips for combining sentences and using syntactic structures, please access the additional resources online (**go.SolutionTree.com/literacy**).

Scaffolding Strategy 25: Analyzing Sentence Structure Using Syntactic Awareness

QUANTITATIVE	QUALITATIVE			
High Lexile	Levels of Meaning	**Structure**	**Language Clarity**	Knowledge Demands

In this strategy, students develop their *syntactic awareness*, which is the "ability to monitor the relationships among the words in a sentence in order to understand while reading or composing orally or in writing" (Sedita, 2020). In other words, syntactic awareness is students' ability to use the parts of a sentence to engage in answering questions like "Who or what did what?" to deconstruct challenging sentences.

Why It Matters

Using syntactic awareness to analyze the structure of individual sentences that make up challenging texts can support developing readers, including MLLs, in improving both their reading fluency and comprehension of the text (Deacon & Kieffer, 2018; Mokhtari & Thompson, 2006; Scott, 2009). This is an effective strategy because many developing readers lack grammatical knowledge or have difficulty processing complex sentence structure, which causes interference in higher-level text comprehension (Martohardjono et al., 2005). Therefore, if you want your developing readers to be able to comprehend more challenging text, then you will need to develop their syntactic awareness.

Often, we don't notice comprehension problems until second or third grade, when the sentences in school texts present language structures that are not typically encountered in everyday language situations (Scott, 2009). Once you engage all students in challenging, grade-level text, you will likely see comprehension issues arise. Spending time helping students look for the relationships among the words in these more complex sentences can mediate those syntactic challenges.

TEACHER TIP

Evidence has shown that MLLs with strong syntactic awareness in their native language demonstrate stronger syntactic awareness in English (Martohardjono et al., 2005). Therefore, it is important that schools support the development of the native language, as doing so will aid in the development of syntactic knowledge in English.

What to Consider Before Implementing

Four main variables have been identified to contribute to sentence complexity (Thompson & Shapiro, 2007).

1. The number of propositions (aligned to the number of verbs in the sentence)
2. The number of *embeddings* (one clause included in another)
3. The order in which the key grammatical elements appear in the sentence (such as active versus passive sentences)
4. The distance between key elements in the sentence (for example, distance between the subject and the predicate)

So, when you preview a text before reading it with your class, you can look for sentences that have these variables and plan for how you might break them down to make them more comprehensible. As you read, you might look for the following: lengthy sentences; sentences where there are several words between the subject and the verb; sentences with connectives like *however*, *despite*, and *although*; sentences with passive voice; or sentences with a pronoun and a referent, where a pronoun is used in place of a previously mentioned character or topic (Gillis & Eberhardt, 2018). All these variables can make a sentence more challenging.

To compensate for these variables, you can help students analyze the sentences using key questions related to the function and form of the words in the sentence. Figure 4.10 contains examples of questions you can use to build syntactic awareness with your students to deconstruct complex sentence structure (Gillis & Eberhardt, 2018).

By asking these questions, you help students break the sentence down into its meaningful parts (such as nouns and verbs) while offering them thinking prompts to help them identify those parts. With practice, students will be able to facilitate this type of thinking independently.

Parts of Speech	Key Questions
Nouns and Pronouns	Who? What?
Verbs	Did what?
Adjectives (including adjectival phrases)	How many? What kind? Which one?
Adverbs (including adverbial phrases)	Where? When? How? Why?

Figure 4.10: Questions to build syntactic awareness.

How to Implement the Strategy

To model how you would use the questions from figure 4.10 to build students' syntactic awareness to assist them in deconstructing complex sentence structure, let's use a passage from the book *Tuck Everlasting* by Natalie Babbitt (2015) as an example. The opening lines read:

> The road that led to Treegap had been trod out long before by a heard of cows who were, to say the least, relaxed. It wandered along in curves and easy angles, swayed off and up in a pleasant tangent to the top of a small hill, ambled down again between fringes of bee-hung clover, and then cut sidewise across a meadow. (Babbitt, 2015, p. 5)

The following is a classroom script demonstrating how to use this strategy, with the questions to facilitate students' syntactic awareness appearing in bold.

[Students echo-read the text, with the teacher serving as the model fluent reader.] (See strategy 11, page 68, for more on echo reading.)

Teacher: *Let's pause there, as those two sentences had a lot of detail in them. Let's take a moment to think about what the sentences convey. Let's start with the first sentence.* **What is the sentence about?**

Gloria: *It is about a road.*

Teacher: *Yes, that is correct. It is about a road.* **What does the road do?**

Nathan: *It led to Treegap, which must be a town since it is capitalized.*

Teacher: *That's good thinking. I agree—I think Treegap is a town. Maybe we will be able to confirm that as we read on. So, the first sentence talks about a road that leads to Treegap.* **What kind of road is it?** *Talk with your elbow partner and use the first sentence to help you decide.*

[Students talk with their partners. Teacher circulates.]

Teacher: *[Signals the class to bring their attention back.] All right, so* **what kind of road is it?**

Melanie: *Tony and I talked about it being like a country road made of dirt.*

Teacher: *Why do you think that? What in the text makes you think so?*

Melanie: *Uh, it talks about cows walking on it, so we thought it must be more in the country.*

Teacher: *OK, so given there are cows walking on it, you think it's a dirt road somewhere in the country. Is that right?*

Melanie: *Yeah.*

Teacher: *Great. Who would like to add on or share a different idea?*

Robert: *We thought it was near a farm or something because of the cows.*

Teacher: *All right, so we think that it is a country or farm road, possibly a dirt road. Well, let's look at the next sentence to see if it gives us any more information about the road.*

[Teacher and students chorally reread the second sentence.]

Teacher: *So, what else do we know about the road now?* **What kind of road is it?** *Turn to your partner and share your thinking.*

[Students talk with their partners. Teacher circulates.]

Teacher: *[Signals the class to bring their attention back.] All right, so what else do we know about* **what kind of road it is?**

Alisa: *It's a winding road.*

Teacher: *What language in the text makes you think that?*

Alisa: *It says "curves" and "swayed" and "ambled down."*

Teacher: *So, those words make you think it is a winding or curvy road?*

Alisa: *Yeah.*

Teacher: *Does anyone else want to add to that?*

Casey: *We think it is a winding road, too, and we still think it is in the country.*

Teacher: *What makes you think that?*

Casey: *It says it cuts across a meadow.*

Teacher: *Oh, and one of the vocabulary words we learned before reading was* meadow. *What does* meadow *mean?*

LaNae: *Land covered in grass.*

Teacher: *That's right. So, right now I am picturing a winding country road that is surrounded by land covered in grass. Anything else you would add?*

Mike: *It sounds like it is hilly.*

Teacher: *What makes you think that?*

Mike: *It says it goes up a small hill and down again. It sounds like the road goes up and down.*

Teacher: *OK, so let's add* hilly. *Now I am picturing a winding dirt road that goes through some small hills of land covered in grass. All right, let's keep reading to see where this road takes us.*

As you can see in this classroom example, by asking those key syntactic questions, we can help students deconstruct complex sentences to increase their comprehension.

How to Practice the Strategy

Choose one to two complex sentences from a text that your students may need some time to deconstruct. In figure 4.11, practice answering the questions you would likely use to help them break the text down into simpler parts.

Who? What?	
Did what?	
How many? What kind? Which one?	
Where? When? How? Why?	

Figure 4.11: Analyzing sentence structure planner.

For more on analyzing sentence structure, including instructional activities to promote syntactic awareness, please access the additional resources online (**go.SolutionTree.com/literacy**).

Chapter Five

Incorporating Scaffolding Strategies Into Instruction

In this chapter, you will explore opportunities to incorporate grade-level text with scaffolding into your whole- and small-group instruction. The first part will explore the varied opportunities for engaging students in grade-level text during Tier 1 (core) instruction across the school day. Then, I will introduce you to a few new ideas on how to support the use of grade-level text in small-group or partner settings while providing scaffolding to improve student success.

Whole-Group Instruction

Any time you engage students in the grade-level curricular materials you have been provided (such as your ELA basal program, science and social studies textbooks, or any other similar materials), those materials are intended to be student texts unless otherwise noted. This means that the students are supposed to do the heavy lifting of reading the texts (Shanahan et al., 2016). So, if you choose to read the text to them, tell them what the text says without using the text, or have them listen to stronger readers in the class read the text, then you won't achieve the intended purpose of those texts. On the contrary, you create inequities by disadvantaging some or all of your students in being able to practice their skills with grade-level material.

There are certainly times in which it is appropriate to read a text aloud (see strategy 8, page 50, for more on reading a text aloud), but if that is your primary strategy for engaging students in the texts they are expected to read, then you won't be providing them with the grade-level experiences desired. Instead, you can use everything you learned in chapters 2–4 to scaffold students in those texts so they can experience them with increased levels of success.

Using Your ELA Core Program Effectively

In most schools, your school district or charter has purchased a literacy program that they expect you to use, not only because of the tremendous financial investment in those materials but also because of the design of such programs. Many core programs in the present day greatly reduce the burden of planning and preparation for the busy educator. Since we now know what our readers most at risk need, core literacy programs can support many of the essential components that are critical for these students. Structured literacy models help us know how important systematic, cumulative instruction is for developing readers (Lyon & Goldberg, 2024). Core materials are systematic because they are organized in a logical, sequential order, with cumulative review built in. This means that, overall, we need to follow the order of the lessons in these programs, as each lesson builds on the previous lessons. If you skip lessons or weeks within a program, you may unintentionally cause gaps in learners' knowledge.

For example, the sequential order of phonics instruction is very intentional in core programs. The authors have considered which letters are most useful to learn first, the instructional spacing between easily confused letters and sounds, and the order of high-frequency words within the series. Therefore, if you skip a week, you might not provide students with enough practice of previously learned skills, or they might miss the introduction of a key phonics skill, or you might unintentionally skip the introduction of specific high-frequency words that subsequent weeks of instruction assume the students have already been exposed to. This is similarly true for text structure development, vocabulary terms, and grammatical skills in a well-designed program. So, given the systematic and cumulative nature of core ELA programs, if you need to skip some parts of instruction for a specific reason, be sure to investigate the scope and sequence to see how you might compensate for what the students will miss.

Not everything in a core program is essential, however. Most programs have way more content than you would ever have time for. This means you will need to select the portions that are essential to reading development. Informed by the findings of the National Reading Panel (2000) and the International Dyslexia Association's recent publication on structured literacy (Lyon & Goldberg, 2024), the following aspects are most critical to developing strong readers.

- Phonemic awareness, particularly blending and segmenting phonemes
- Phonics, including the alphabetic principle, decoding, morphemic analysis, syllable and stress patterns, and word work
- Fluency, including accuracy, rate, and expression
- Vocabulary and background knowledge
- Comprehension
- Sentence structure and grammar
- Orthographic (writing) conventions
- Text structure
- Critical thinking

As you examine your ELA core materials, look for these components and prioritize your instruction accordingly. Any other aspects that do not directly relate to these components are not critical, so rest assured, you do not need to teach them to get results. As a teacher, you must be a wise consumer and use your professional knowledge to make the best instructional decisions for your students. Core literacy programs are built for the average student, and you do not have a classroom of average students; therefore, you need to bring your students' needs to the materials and take what you know about the science of reading and reading instruction to plan, deliver, and modify your teaching to maximize student learning.

To practice this, locate your ELA core program's scope and sequence, which may be in the individual teacher editions or its own separate resource. It may be easier to find it in the digital materials than to locate the actual text, depending on how many years it has been since your last core adoption. Using figure 5.1, take some time, maybe even with your grade-level team, to identify which elements of your core program are essential, which elements are missing, and which elements are not necessary.

Essential Components	Present in Materials	Missing in Materials
Phonemic awareness, particularly blending and segmenting phonemes (grades K–1)		
Phonics, including the alphabetic principle, decoding, morphemic analysis, syllable and stress patterns, and word work		
Fluency, including accuracy, rate, and expression		
Vocabulary and background knowledge		
Comprehension		
Sentence structure and grammar		
Orthographic (writing) conventions		
Text structure		
Critical thinking		

Figure 5.1: Essential ELA core instruction components.
*Visit **go.SolutionTree.com/literacy** for a free reproducible version of this figure.*

Delivering Explicit Instruction Effectively

Knowing the aspects of the program to use and understanding the intentionality of the design and order of lessons are just part of the story. The other side is the need for delivering ELA instruction effectively. Unlike in mathematics and science, where an inquiry approach may be more effective at times, literacy instruction requires a more direct approach. We don't ask students to guess what the letter *b* sounds like—we tell them and have them practice it. In our initial introduction to the letter *b*, we don't ask them to tell us words that begin with *b*—we give them examples, and maybe even some nonexamples, of words that begin with *b*. We must be explicit. Explicit instruction is critical for meeting the needs of all learners (Archer & Hughes, 2011; Lyon & Goldberg, 2024).

Explicit instruction is most commonly known as the *I Do, We Do, You Do* model, which uses a gradual release to develop students' capacity over time. Although the gradual release model is a critical part of explicit instruction, there are several embedded practices that you must integrate to make explicit instruction highly effective. In particular, as represented in figure 5.2, there are four explicit instructional techniques that can increase your impact on student learning (Archer & Hughes, 2011; Carnine, Silbert, Kame'enui, Tarver, & Jungjohann, 2006).

Explicit Instruction Techniques	Description
Prompt, corrective feedback	The teacher acknowledges students' errors by pointing out the error, explaining how to fix it, and giving them the opportunity to do it correctly with supported practice that the teacher delivers immediately following the error.
Monitoring	The teacher circulates the room during independent practice to monitor students' responses and provide brief feedback as needed to support students in building automaticity with the skill they're developing.
Pacing	The teacher presents the content and solicits students' responses at a brisk pace to allow time for students to think and process the information while maintaining high levels of engagement and maximizing instructional time.
Signaling	The teacher uses gesturing to make it clear to students when to respond to foster a learning environment in which all students create their own responses and don't rely on mimicking others to do so. For example, during whole-word blending, the teacher points to the side of the word to be read and says, "Think," then after a few seconds, moves their finger to point under the word and says, "Read." Students respond in unison by reading the word.

Figure 5.2: *Explicit instruction techniques.*

By using these techniques for explicit instruction whenever introducing new literacy concepts or developing students' accuracy and automaticity in literacy knowledge and skills, you will see improved results in student learning (Archer & Hughes, 2011; Carnine et al., 2006).

Building Knowledge in the Content Areas

Beyond reading texts within your ELA core materials, you will also want to provide a healthy diet of content-rich reading experiences across content areas, like in social studies, science, health, and the arts. There is a growing body of research that shows the impact that knowledge has on students' reading comprehension (Tyner & Kabourek, 2021; Wexler, 2019, 2021). Students comprehend text better when they have knowledge of the topic.

Unfortunately, as a byproduct of the No Child Left Behind Act (2002), we have seen a mass reduction in elementary schools giving their attention to subjects other than literacy and mathematics (Heafner & Fitchett, 2012). This has likely contributed to static literacy achievement scores because, as Tina L. Heafner and Paul G. Fitchett's (2012) research demonstrates, ensuring students have previous knowledge of the topic they're reading greatly improves the likelihood that they will be able to comprehend at high levels. So, if you want to grow your readers, you need to expand their knowledge of the world and build their knowledge banks more broadly. Don't forget that you can attend to critical aspects of literacy development like text structure, critical thinking, vocabulary, and sentence structure in texts outside of the ELA curriculum. In fact, often, our discipline-specific texts are prime resources to do just that (Shanahan & Shanahan, 2012). I encourage you to bring a wider range of subjects back to your classrooms!

Small-Group and Partner Instruction

Now, let's consider the implications of using grade-level text in small-group and partner settings. First, let's define small-group instruction. For this book, *small-group instruction* refers to instruction in which you work with a subset of students in your class to address a specific need. Generally, you might use small groups to provide more personalized instruction for students who:

- Demonstrate the need for more practice or more instruction based on their responses or performance in core instruction
- Have specific, skill-based learning needs as identified by formative assessment practices like diagnostic assessment, benchmark data, progress-monitoring data, ELA program assessments, or teacher observation data

Depending on the students' needs, small-group instruction is a great way to provide additional instruction in grade-level text that can be even more explicit, structured, and scaffolded based on grade-level concepts, ideas, and vocabulary, thus supporting students in meeting grade-level expectations.

Using challenging, grade-level texts in combination with the scaffolding strategies in this book is effective in not only whole-group instruction but small-group instruction as well. You may use any of the twenty-five scaffolding strategies presented herein as scaffolded supports when working with small groups of students, yet the advantage of smaller settings is they allow you more opportunities to personalize the strategies than what might be possible in the whole-group setting.

Beyond the scaffolding strategies already presented, there are three related instructional practices you may consider employing in a small-group setting that can be particularly effective for accelerating students' reading growth in grade-level text: front-loading key vocabulary, concepts, and skills; using partners as a scaffold with dyad reading; and using repeated reading.

Front-loading Key Vocabulary, Concepts, and Skills

Front-loading is defined as the intentional exposure of vocabulary, concepts, and skills that you will use in instruction in the coming hours or days (Marzano, 2004). This powerful approach serves as a mechanism for supporting developing readers in accessing grade-level instruction by using small-group instruction time to preview essential content that you will teach in core instruction in the upcoming days. Specifically, front-loading the vocabulary and background knowledge students will need for a text using chunking, scaffolding, or visual cues is effective for preparing developing readers for fuller engagement and opportunity in grade-level text instruction (Zheng, 2012).

Some example ways in which you can front-load and prepare students to more successfully and meaningfully engage in grade-level text include the following.

- **Images or video clips:** Provide pictures or a short video clip that gives visual cues about the concepts in the text. Discuss the pictures and their connection to the topic and content of the text. This could include previewing the text and examining the images, charts, tables, and other visuals found within the text, too.

- **Explicit vocabulary instruction routine:** Select key terms that are most critical for conceptual understanding related to the text and front-load them using the explicit vocabulary instruction routine like the one in figure 2.9 (page 37).

- **Concept map:** Work with students to curate their prior knowledge about the topic they will be studying and create a concept map with the key concepts. You may need to provide the key categories for the concept map to foster students' thinking. (For more on concept maps, revisit strategy 14, page 84.)

○ **Simpler text:** Find lower-level text that you can use to introduce the topic with less complex and challenging text. Engage students in reading the simpler text and processing their learning by asking questions, discussing the key concepts, adding to a concept map, and so on.

The idea is to support developing readers, including MLLs, by preparing for what they will encounter in their reading. Identifying students in your class who could benefit from developing their vocabulary on and knowledge of the topic in the text will make this strategy most effective.

Using Partners as a Scaffold With Dyad Reading

Dyad reading is a reading intervention for grades 2 and up that is based on the neurological impress method. In R. G. Heckelman's (1969) original design, an adult tutor pairs with a developing reader. The adult tutor and developing reader chorally read a challenging text, yielding an average increase of two grade levels after seven and a half hours of intervention (Heckelman, 1969). Then, in 1988, J. Lloyd Eldredge and D. William Quinn amended the method to use student pairings instead, allowing for the practice to be used in a whole-group setting. Using a more proficient peer as the scaffold instead of an adult resulted in learning outcomes comparable to those in Heckelman's (1969) research. Dyad reading is effective because it provides a developing reader with scaffolded access to hear, see, and say the words in a challenging text through choral reading with a more fluent reader, ultimately improving their sight recognition of words over time (Dougherty Stahl, 2012).

Teachers can employ dyad reading with parent volunteers, during small-group instruction as a center (once they have established routines), or as a whole-group strategy. Teachers have used it in small-group instruction to replace practices like silent sustained reading (or, as I call it, "silent sustained staring"). Dyad reading has built-in accountability given the student partnership and the choral reading students engage in that the teacher can actively monitor.

To implement dyad reading, establishing effective reading partnerships and selecting appropriately challenging texts are the two most important components for success. To establish strategic partnerships, please follow the detailed description found in strategy 11 (page 68). To select the right texts, use the developing reader's current independent reading level to find a text that is at least two years above their level (Brown et al., 2014).

In table 5.1 (page 148), Lexile levels are aligned to grade levels. You can use a student's current Lexile level and this chart to identify what level of text is at least two grade levels above. For example, if a second-grade developing reader's Lexile is 180L (first-grade reading level), then two grade levels above that is 645L (third-grade reading level).

Table 5.1: Lexile Chart by Grade Level

Grade Level	Lexile Level 50th Percentile
Kindergarten	BR160L
1st Grade	165L
2nd Grade	425L
3rd Grade	645L
4th Grade	850L
5th Grade	950L
6th Grade	1030L

Source: Mohawk Valley Community College Libraries, 2023.

Find Appropriately Challenging Text

Once you know your desired level of text difficulty for your students (two years above their independent reading level), you need to find texts that are interesting, motivating, and, most importantly, appropriately challenging; a critical feature of dyad reading is challenging text. You won't see the same level of acceleration in reading progress if you don't assign students text that is two years above their current Lexile level. It isn't that you won't see any progress—you just won't see the expected results. Appropriately challenging is key!

To determine which books might work best for each student pair, you can use tools like Find a Book (https://hub.lexile.com/find-a-book/search) to search for potential titles and identify their Lexile levels. You might want to leverage a student's parent or a school volunteer to help with this. You can set them up on a website like this and have them label and organize the books in your classroom library by Lexile level, which will make your book assignments more efficient.

Once you find books at the appropriate Lexile level, it's time to pick out three to five books for each partnership. The benefit of providing more than one book for each partnership is it provides students with some choice in what they read and allows them to gravitate to the books that best match their interests. This is where knowing about your students is extremely valuable. Perhaps you have a student who loves reading about animals—then you might want to include at least one book that is about animals. You can store each partnership's reading material in a gallon-sized plastic bag or in a book bin to make it easy for them to grab their materials when it is dyad reading time.

Once you have initiated dyad reading and students have finished reading their first book, you can send them over to your classroom library to pick out their next book using their designated Lexile level. This will reduce the ongoing burden of choosing texts for your students, and it empowers the students to select their own books within the appropriate Lexile level. Also, keep in mind that students will make progress across the year, so be sure to use your assessment data to keep increasing the text difficulty as students demonstrate greater proficiency.

Learn Dyad Reading Partner Principles

Now that you have established partnerships, determined the appropriately challenging Lexile level, and selected texts for the pair to use, it is time to train the partners on the dyad reading partner principles (Brown et al., 2014), which are as follows.

1. Sit side by side.
2. Share one book.
3. Track words with one smooth finger.
4. Keep eyes on the text.
5. Ensure two voices are reading at a conversational pace.
6. Have fun!

Explicitly modeling, training, and providing ongoing feedback on students' implementation of these principles will foster effective dyad reading conditions to yield the desired results. Partners should engage in these principles for about fifteen minutes per day. Providing a reminder of the principles, like the bookmark in figure 5.3, can be a great way to refer students to them when providing students with feedback on their practice. In the beginning, you may need to start with fewer minutes as students build up their stamina, working your way up to fifteen minutes. Having personally seen dyad reading done in numerous classrooms, I know that students get excited for it, and it becomes one of their favorite parts of the day!

Using Repeated Reading

Repeated reading is an evidence-based technique that can be used after the initial reading of the text. It involves students rereading a text they have previously read. The body of evidence consistently shows that students who engage in repeated reading demonstrate marked increases in their fluency and comprehension (Gorsuch & Taguchi, 2010; Therrien, 2004). It has been found to be effective for all types of students, including students with disabilities and MLLs.

Figure 5.3: Dyad reading partner principles bookmark.

*Visit **go.SolutionTree.com/literacy** for a free reproducible version of this figure.*

So, after you have initially read the text during whole-group instruction, in small group, you can organize a group of students who would benefit from rereading the text to improve their reading fluency as well as their comprehension. You can do this on a daily or weekly basis and make it part of your differentiated, small-group instruction time, or you can use repeated reading with texts that you intend for students to engage with beyond the initial exposure, such as by writing essays, holding a class discussion or debate, and so on. When you engage students in repeated reading, you give them the opportunity to reread the entire text up to three more times (if it is short) or key portions of the text (if it is long).

To motivate students to engage in the same text multiple times, you will want to incorporate one or more of the six active reading engagement techniques (cloze reading, choral reading, partner reading, and so on) into your instruction. (See strategy 11, page 68, for more information on active reading engagement techniques.) You can list the six techniques on a sheet of paper and have students take turns picking which active reading technique they want to use for that page, section, or paragraph. You can also roll a die to select which technique to use, with each number on the dice corresponding to one of the six techniques (see figure 5.4). Little moves like this empower student voice and gamify the lesson a bit.

Figure 5.4: Active reading engagement small-group chart.

Visit **go.SolutionTree.com/literacy** *for a free reproducible version of this figure.*

As you're engaging students in rereading the text using active engagement techniques, be sure to stop throughout to ask questions and discuss their understanding of the text. Each reading will yield deeper and deeper levels of understanding, so plan the rigor of your questions accordingly. If you have assigned a writing task or are planning a more in-depth class discussion as a next step to the text, this can be a great time to work on note-taking or to use a graphic organizer for students to collect the details they may want to incorporate into their writing or the discussion. Think of this time as additional scaffolded practice reading the text as well as an opportunity to scaffold connected learning activities that you want to be able to provide more explicit supports for.

To practice this, given the small-group and partnership ideas presented, reflect on which of these three approaches you are interested in trying out in your own classroom: (1) front-loading key vocabulary, concepts, and skills; (2) using partners as a scaffold with dyad reading; and (3) using repeated reading. Consider the following questions to help you decide.

- What are the needs of my students?
- Which idea would best meet their needs? (For example, students developing their English proficiency would benefit from front-loading key vocabulary, concepts, and skills.)
- What resources or time would I need to dedicate to incorporating the idea? (For example, you would need to establish strategic partnerships, obtain data on students' reading levels, and find books with the appropriate Lexile levels to use the dyad reading approach.)
- Do I have students who would benefit from improving their reading rate and accuracy in grade-level text?
- How might I incorporate repeated reading into my instructional routine?

Now that you have read about the robust evidence base that demonstrates that you can expect more dramatic increases in reading proficiency when engaging students in grade-level text, learned about the scaffolding strategies you can use to support all students in grade-level text, and explored ideas for when and how to incorporate grade-level text into your daily instruction, you are ready to transform your students' reading progress and watch them thrive through your strong instructional moves. As you implement what you have learned in this book, come back to reread sections that you need to revisit for deeper understanding and clarification or to refresh your memory.

By believing that all students can access grade-level text and incorporating one scaffolding strategy at a time, you will quickly see your grade-level text scaffolding tool kit expand and your students' success grow. Enjoy the journey of seeing accelerated progress for your students!

REFERENCES AND RESOURCES

Adams, G. N. (2008, January 14). *Written expression: Building the foundation in primary grades* [Conference presentation]. SSTAGE Conference, Athens, GA, United States.

Adams, M. J. (2010–2011). Advancing our students' language and literacy: The challenge of complex texts. *American Educator, 34*(4), 3–11.

Ajideh, P. (2006). Schema-theory based considerations on pre-reading activities in ESP textbooks. *Asian EFL Journal, 16*, 1–19.

Alexander, P. A., Kulikowich, J. M., & Schulze, S. K. (1994). How subject-matter knowledge affects recall and interest. *American Educational Research Journal, 31*(2), 313–337.

Alfaki, I. M., & Siddiek, A. G. (2013). The role of background knowledge in enhancing reading comprehension. *World Journal of English Language, 3*(4), 42–66.

Allington, R. L. (2002, November). You can't learn much from books you can't read. *Educational Leadership, 60*(3).

Allington, R. L. (2005, June/July). The other five "pillars" of effective reading instruction. *Reading Today, 22*(6), 3.

Almasi, J. F. (2002). Peer discussion. In B. Guzzetti (Ed.), *Literacy in America: An encyclopedia of history, theory and practice* (Vol. 2). ABC-CLIO.

Almasi, J. F., & Garas-York, K. (2009). Comprehension and discussion of text. In S. E. Israel & G. G. Duffy (Eds.), *Handbook of research on reading comprehension* (pp. 470–493). Routledge.

Amer, A. A. (1997). The effect of the teacher's reading aloud on the reading comprehension of EFL students. *ELT Journal, 51*(1), 43–47.

Anderson, V., & Hidi, S. (1988–1989, December/January). Teaching students to summarize. *Educational Leadership, 46*(4), 26–28.

Archer, A. L., & Hughes, C. A. (2011). *Explicit instruction: Effective and efficient teaching*. Guilford Press.

Arfé, B., Mason, L., & Fajardo, I. (2018). Simplifying informational text structure for struggling readers. *Reading and Writing: An Interdisciplinary Journal, 31*(9), 2191–2210.

Armbruster, B., Anderson, T. H., & Ostertag, J. (1987). Does text structure/summarization instruction facilitate learning from expository text? *Reading Research Quarterly, 22*(3), 331–346.

Armbruster, B., Lehr, F., & Osborn, J. (2001). *Put reading first: The research building blocks for teaching children to read.* Government Printing Office. Accessed at www.nichd.nih.gov/publications/product/239 on February 25, 2025.

Asaro-Saddler, K., Muir-Knox, H., & Meredith, H. (2018). The effects of a summary writing strategy on the literacy skills of adolescents with disabilities. *Exceptionality, 26*(2), 106–118.

August, D., Carlo, M., Dressler, C., & Snow, C. (2005). The critical role of vocabulary development for English language learners. *Learning Disabilities Research and Practice, 20*(1), 50–57.

Ausubel, D. P. (1963). *The psychology of meaningful verbal learning: An introduction to school learning.* Grune & Stratton.

Averette, P. (n.d.). *Save the last word for ME.* Accessed at www.schoolreforminitiative.org/download/save-the-last-word-for-me/?wpdmdl=12588&refresh=66d0e6d45b7411724966612 on November 5, 2024.

Babbitt, N. (2015). *Tuck everlasting* (40th anniversary ed.). Farrar, Straus, Giroux.

Baer, E. (1992). *This is the way we go to school: A book about children around the world* (S. Björkman, Illus.). Scholastic.

Barko-Alva, K., & Chang-Bacon, C. (2023). Over-framing: Interrogating sentence frames as pedagogical support vs. language restriction. *Language, Culture and Curriculum, 36*(4), 422–438.

Baumann, J. F. (2009). Intensity in vocabulary instruction and effects on reading comprehension. *Topics in Language Disorders, 29*(4), 312–328.

Bean, T. W., Singer, H., Sorter, J., & Frazee, C. (1986). The effect of metacognitive instruction in outlining and graphic organizer construction on students' comprehension in a tenth-grade world history class. *Journal of Reading Behavior, 18*(2), 153–169.

Beck, I. L., McKeown, M. G., & Kucan, L. (2002). *Bringing words to life: Robust vocabulary instruction.* Guilford Press.

Beck, I. L., McKeown, M. G., & Kucan, L. (2013). *Bringing words to life: Robust vocabulary instruction* (2nd ed.). Guilford Press.

Begeny, J. C., Krouse, H. E., Ross, S. G., & Mitchell, R. C. (2009). Increasing elementary-aged students' reading fluency with small-group interventions: A comparison of repeated reading, listening passage preview, and listening only strategies. *Journal of Behavioral Education, 18*(3), 211–228.

Bessette, H. J. (2020). Using choral reading to improve reading fluency of students with exceptionalities. *Georgia Journal of Literacy, 43*(2), Article 4.

Betts, E. A. (1946). *Foundations of reading instruction.* American Book Company.

Blachman, B. A., Schatschneider, C., Fletcher, J. M., Francis, D. J., Clonan, S. M., Shaywitz, B. A., et al. (2004). Effects of intensive reading remediation for second and third graders and a 1-year follow-up. *Journal of Educational Psychology, 96*(3), 444–461.

Bogaerds-Hazenberg, S. T. M., Evers-Vermeul, J., & van den Bergh, H. (2021). A meta-analysis on the effects of text structure instruction on reading comprehension in the upper elementary grades. *Reading Research Quarterly, 56*(3), 435–462.

Brandenburg, M. L. (2002). Advanced math? Write! *Educational Leadership, 60*(3), 67–68.

Bransford, J. D. (1979). *Human cognition: Learning, understanding, and remembering.* Wadsworth.

Bray Donnelly, W., & Roe, C. J. (2010). Using sentence frames to develop academic vocabulary for English learners. *The Reading Teacher, 64*(2), 131–136.

Bridges, D. (1979). *Education, democracy, and discussion.* Humanities Press.

Brody, S. (Ed.). (2001). *Teaching reading: Language, letters and thought* (2nd ed.). LARC.

Brown, A. L., Ash, D., Rutherford, M., Nakagawa, K., Gordon, A., & Campione, J. C. (1993). Distributed expertise in the classroom. In G. Salomon (Ed.), *Distributed cognitions: Psychological and educational considerations* (pp. 188–228). Cambridge University Press.

Brown, A. L., Campione, J. C., & Day, J. D. (1981). Learning to learn: On training students to learn from texts. *Educational Researcher, 10*(2), 14–21.

Brown, P. C., Roediger, H. L., III, & McDaniel, M. A. (2014). *Make it stick: The science of successful learning.* Belknap Press.

Burns, M. K. (2007). Reading at the instructional level with children identified as learning disabled: Potential implications for response-to-intervention. *School Psychology Quarterly, 22*(3), 297–313.

Burns, M. K. (2024). Assessing an instructional level during reading fluency interventions: A meta-analysis of the effects on reading. *Assessment for Effective Intervention, 49*(4), 214–224. https://doi.org/10.1177/15345084241247064

Carnes, E. R., Lindbeck, J. S., & Griffin, C. F. (1987). Effects of group size and advance organizers on learning parameters when using microcomputer tutorials in kinematics. *Journal of Research in Science Teaching, 24*(9), 781–789.

Carnine, D. W., Silbert, J., Kame'enui, E. J., Tarver, S. G., & Jungjohann, K. (2006). *Teaching struggling and at-risk readers: A direct instruction approach.* Merrill/Prentice Hall.

Casteel, C. A. (1988). Effects of chunked reading among learning disabled students: An experimental comparison of computer and traditional chunked passages. *Journal of Educational Technology Systems, 17*(2), 115–121.

Casteel, C. A. (1990). Effects of chunked text-material on reading comprehension of high and low ability readers. *Reading Improvement, 27*(4), 269–275.

Cervetti, G., & Barber, J. (2009). Bringing back books. *Science and Children, 47*(3), 36–39.

Cervetti, G., Wright, T. S., & Hwang, H. (2016). Conceptual coherence, comprehension, and vocabulary acquisition: A knowledge effect? *Reading and Writing: An Interdisciplinary Journal, 29*(4), 761–779.

Chall, J. S., Jacobs, V. A., & Baldwin, L. E. (1990). *The reading crisis: Why poor children fall behind.* Harvard University Press.

Chang, A. C.-S., & Millett, S. (2015). Improving reading rates and comprehension through audio-assisted extensive reading for beginner learners. *System, 52*, 91–102.

Cheatham, J. P., & Allor, J. H. (2012). The influence of decodability in early reading text on reading achievement: A review of the evidence. *Reading and Writing: An Interdisciplinary Journal, 25*(9), 2223–2246.

Chesebro, J. L., & McCroskey, J. C. (2001). The relationship of teacher clarity and immediacy with student state receiver apprehension, affect and cognitive learning. *Communication Education, 50*(1), 59–68.

Clements-Davis, G. L., & Ley, T. C. (1991). Thematic preorganizers and the reading comprehension of tenth-grade world literature students. *Reading Research and Instruction, 31*(1), 43–53.

Clinton-Lisell, V. (2023). Does reading while listening to text improve comprehension compared to reading only? A systematic review and meta-analysis. *Educational Research: Theory and Practice, 34*(3), 133–155.

Collins, J. L., & Madigan, T. P. (2010). Using writing to develop struggling learners' higher level reading comprehension. In J. L. Collins & T. G. Gunning (Eds.), *Building struggling students' higher level literacy: Practical ideas, powerful solutions* (pp. 103–124). International Reading Association.

Collins, S. (2008). *The hunger games*. Scholastic Press.

Colliot, T., & Jamet, É. (2019). Asking students to be active learners: The effects of totally or partially self-generating a graphic organizer on students' learning performances. *Instructional Science, 47*(4), 463–480.

Colorín Colorado. (n.d.). *Sentence frames and sentence starters*. Accessed at www.colorincolorado.org/sentence-frames on November 5, 2024.

Cummins, S. (2017, February). The case for multiple texts. *Educational Leadership, 74*(5), 66–71.

Cunningham, A. E., & Stanovich, K. E. (1997). Early reading acquisition and its relation to reading experience and ability 10 years later. *Developmental Psychology, 33*(6), 934–945.

Darch, C., & Eaves, R. C. (1986). Visual displays to increase comprehension of high school learning-disabled students. *The Journal of Special Education, 20*(3), 309–318.

Deacon, S. H., & Kieffer, M. (2018). Understanding how syntactic awareness contributes to reading comprehension: Evidence from mediation and longitudinal models. *Journal of Educational Psychology, 110*(1), 72–86.

Diakidoy, I.-A. N., Stylianou, P., Karefillidou, C., & Papageorgiou, P. (2005). The relationship between listening and reading comprehension of different types of text at increasing grade levels. *Reading Psychology, 26*(1), 55–80.

Dollins, C. (2011). Comprehending expository texts: Scaffolding students through writing summaries. *California Reader, 45*(2), 22–28.

Dougherty Stahl, K. A. (2012). Complex text or frustration-level text: Using shared reading to bridge the difference. *The Reading Teacher, 66*(1), 47–51.

Dougherty Stahl, K. A. (2014). New insights about letter learning. *The Reading Teacher, 68*(4), 261–265.

D'Souza, K. (2022, November 14). "Just-right" books: Does leveled reading hurt the weakest readers? *EdSource*. Accessed at https://edsource.org/2022/just-right-books-does-leveled-reading-hurt-the-weakest-readers/680958 on November 6, 2024.

Duke, N. K. (2000). 3.6 minutes per day: The scarcity of informational texts in first grade. *Reading Research Quarterly, 35*(2), 202–224.

Duke, N. K. (2004, March). The case for informational text. *Educational Leadership, 61*(6), 40–44.

Duke, N. K., & Mesmer, H. A. E. (2018–2019, Winter). Phonics faux pas: Avoiding instructional missteps in teaching letter-sound relationships. *American Educator, 42*(4), 12–16.

Dwiana, N. R. (2023). The use of sketch-to-stretch strategy to improve students' listening comprehension. *Global Expert: Jurnal Bahasa dan Sastra*, *11*(2), 70–74.

Educators for Excellence. (2024). *Voices from the classroom: A survey of America's educators*. Author. Accessed at https://e4e.org/wp-content/uploads/2024/05/2024-Voices-from-the-Classroom-Report.pdf on November 6, 2024.

Eeds, M., & Wells, D. (1989). Grand conversations: An exploration of meaning construction in literature study groups. *Research in the Teaching of English*, *23*(1), 4–29.

Ehri, L. C., & Sweet, J. (1991). Fingerpoint-reading of memorized text: What enables beginners to process the print? *Reading Research Quarterly*, *26*(4), 442–462.

Eldredge, J. L., & Quinn, D. W. (1988). Increasing reading performance of low-achieving second graders with dyad reading groups. *The Journal of Educational Research*, *82*(1), 40–46.

Ellery, V. (2005). *Creating strategic readers: Techniques for developing competency in phonemic awareness, phonics, fluency, vocabulary, and comprehension*. International Literacy Association.

Ellis, E. (2004). *Q&A: What's the big deal with graphic organizers?* Accessed at www.scribd.com/document/140226323/Q-and-a-About-Graphic-Organizers on February 25, 2025.

Estebo, R. (2012). *How does paragraph shrinking affect reading comprehension of struggling intermediate students?* [Unpublished master's thesis]. Southwest Minnesota State University.

Esteves, K. J., & Whitten, E. (2011). Assisted reading with digital audiobooks for students with reading disabilities. *Reading Horizons*, *51*(1), 21–40.

Everett, S., & Moyer, R. (2009). Methods and strategies: Literacy in the learning cycle. *Science and Children*, *47*(2), 48–52.

Facing History and Ourselves. (2008, February 24). *Graffiti boards*. Accessed at www.facinghistory.org/resource-library/teaching-strategies/graffiti-boards on February 27, 2022.

Fisher, D., & Frey, N. (2014). Scaffolded reading instruction of content-area texts. *The Reading Teacher*, *67*(5), 347–351.

Fisher, D., Frey, N., Almarode, J., Barbee, K., Amador, O., & Assof, J. (2024). *The teacher clarity playbook, grades K–12: A hands-on guide to creating learning intentions and success criteria for organized, effective instruction* (2nd ed.). Corwin Press.

Fisher, D., Frey, N., & Shanahan, T. (2012, March). The challenge of challenging text. *Educational Leadership*, *69*(6), 58–62.

Foorman, B., Beyler, N., Borradaile, K., Coyne, M., Denton, C. A., Dimino, J., et al. (2016, July). *Foundational skills to support reading for understanding in kindergarten through 3rd grade* (NCEE 2016-4008) [Report]. National Center for Education Evaluation and Regional Assistance. Accessed at https://ies.ed.gov/ncee/WWC/Docs/PracticeGuide/wwc_foundationalreading_040717.pdf on November 5, 2024.

Foorman, B., Francis, D. J., Fletcher, J. M., Schatschneider, C., & Mehta, P. (1998). The role of instruction in learning to read: Preventing reading failure in at-risk children. *Journal of Educational Psychology*, *90*(1), 37–55.

Fordham, N. W., Wellman, D., & Sandmann, A. (2002). Taming the text: Engaging and supporting students in social studies readings. *The Social Studies*, *93*(4), 149–158.

Fraser, B. J., Walberg, H. J., Welch, W. W., & Hattie, J. A. (1987). Syntheses of educational productivity research. *International Journal of Educational Research*, *11*(2), 147–252.

Frechtling, J. A., Zhang, X., & Silverstein, G. (2006). The Voyager Universal Literacy System: Results from a study of kindergarten students in inner-city schools. *Journal of Education for Students Placed at Risk, 11*(1), 75–95.

Fuchs, D., Fuchs, L. S., & Burish, P. (2000). Peer-Assisted Learning Strategies: An evidence-based practice to promote reading achievement. *Learning Disabilities Research and Practice, 15*(2), 85–91.

Fuchs, D., Fuchs, L. S., Mathes, P. G., & Simmons, D. C. (1997). Peer-assisted learning strategies: Making classrooms more responsive to diversity. *American Educational Research Journal, 34*(1), 174–206.

Garrison, S. (2016, September 23). *What are "text sets," and why use them in the classroom?* Accessed at https://fordhaminstitute.org/national/commentary/what-are-text-sets-and-why-use-them-classroom on November 6, 2024.

Gickling, E. E., & Armstrong, D. L. (1978). Levels of instructional difficulty as related to on-task behavior, task completion, and comprehension. *Journal of Learning Disabilities, 11*(9), 559–566.

Gillis, M. B., & Eberhardt, N. C. (2018). *Syntax: Knowledge to practice*. Literacy How.

Gorsuch, G., & Taguchi, E. (2010). Developing reading fluency and comprehension using repeated reading: Evidence from longitudinal student reports. *Language Teaching Research, 14*(1), 27–59.

Graham, S., & Hebert, M. (2010). *Writing to read: Evidence for how writing can improve reading* [Report]. Alliance for Excellent Education. Accessed at www.readingrockets.org/sites/default/files/2023-07/ccny_report_2010_writing-to-read.pdf on November 6, 2024.

Graham, S., & Perin, D. (2007). *Writing next: Effective strategies to improve writing of adolescents in middle and high schools* [Report]. Alliance for Excellent Education. Accessed at https://media.carnegie.org/filer_public/3c/f5/3cf58727-34f4-4140-a014-723a00ac56f7/ccny_report_2007_writing.pdf on November 6, 2024.

Graves, M. F., Cooke, C. L., & Laberge, M. J. (1983). Effects of previewing difficult short stories on low ability junior high school students' comprehension, recall, and attitudes. *Reading Research Quarterly, 18*(3), 262–276.

Grifhorst, J., Lessway, J., & Zamborowski, M. (2012). Alternative to round robin reading. *Michigan Reading Journal, 44*(2), Article 6.

Hacker, D. J., & Tenent, A. (2002). Implementing reciprocal teaching in the classroom: Overcoming obstacles and making modifications. *Journal of Educational Psychology, 94*(4), 699–718.

Hall, L. A. (2012). The role of reading identities and reading abilities in students' discussions about texts and comprehension strategies. *Journal of Literacy Research, 44*(3), 239–272.

Harste, J. C., & Short, K. G. (1988). *Creating classrooms for authors: The reading-writing connection*. Heinemann.

Hasbrouck, J. (2010). *Developing fluent readers* [White paper]. Read Naturally. Accessed at www.readnaturally.com/article/developing-fluent-readers-white-paper on November 6, 2024.

Hattan, C., Alexander, P. A., & Lupo, S. M. (2024). Leveraging what students know to make sense of texts: What the research says about prior knowledge activation. *Review of Educational Research, 94*(1), 73–111.

Heafner, T. L., & Fitchett, P. G. (2012). Tipping the scales: National trends of declining social studies instructional time in elementary schools. *Journal of Social Studies Research, 36*(2), 190–215.

Hebert, M., Bohaty, J. J., Nelson, J. R., & Brown, J. (2016). The effects of text structure instruction on expository reading comprehension: A meta-analysis. *Journal of Educational Psychology, 108*(5), 609–629.

Hebert, M., Graham, S., Rigby-Wills, H., & Ganson, K. (2014). Effects of note-taking and extended writing on expository text comprehension: Who benefits? *Learning Disabilities: A Contemporary Journal, 12*(1), 43–68.

Hebert, M., Simpson, A., & Graham, S. (2013). Comparing effects of different writing activities on reading comprehension: A meta-analysis. *Reading and Writing: An Interdisciplinary Journal, 26*(1), 111–138.

Heckelman, R. G. (1969). A neurological-impress method of remedial-reading instruction. *Academic Therapy, 4*(4), 277–282.

Hidi, S., & Anderson, V. (1986). Producing written summaries: Task demands, cognitive operations, and implications for instruction. *Review of Educational Research, 56*(4), 473–493.

Hiebert, E. H., & Raphael, T. E. (1998). *Early literacy instruction*. Harcourt Brace College.

Hiebert, J., & Wearne, D. (1993). Instructional tasks, classroom discourse, and students' learning in second grade arithmetic. *American Educational Research Journal, 30*(2), 393–425.

Hochman, J. C., & Wexler, N. (2017). *The writing revolution: A guide to advancing thinking through writing in all subjects and grades*. Jossey-Bass.

Honig, B., Diamond, L., & Gutlohn, L. (2018). *Teaching reading sourcebook* (3rd ed.). Academic Therapy.

Hoskisson, K., & Krohm, B. (1974). Reading by immersion: Assisted reading. *Elementary English, 51*(6), 832–836.

Izzati, K. A. (2023). The effectiveness of partner reading strategy on students' reading comprehension. *Journal of English Language and Education, 8*(1), 75–83.

Jenkins, J. R., Peyton, J. A., Sanders, E. A., & Vadasy, P. F. (2004). Effects of reading decodable texts in supplemental first-grade tutoring. *Scientific Studies of Reading, 8*(1), 53–85.

Jenkins, S., & Page, R. (2003). *What do you do with a tail like this?* Houghton Mifflin.

Jiang, X., & Grabe, W. (2007). Graphic organizers in reading instruction: Research findings and issues. *Reading in a Foreign Language, 19*(1), 34–55.

Johnson, K., & Lapp, D. (2012). If you want students to read widely and well—eliminate round-robin reading. In D. Lapp & B. Moss (Eds.), *Exemplary instruction in the middle grades: Teaching that supports engagement and rigorous learning* (pp. 260–273). Guilford Press.

Kansızoğlu, H. B. (2017). The effect of graphic organizers on language teaching and learning areas: A meta-analysis study. *Education and Science, 42*(191), 139–164.

Katayama, A. D., & Robinson, D. H. (2000). Getting students "partially" involved in note-taking using graphic organizers. *The Journal of Experimental Education, 68*(2), 119–133.

Kim, A.-H., Vaughn, S., Wanzek, J., & Wei, S. (2004). Graphic organizers and their effects on the reading comprehension of students with LD: A synthesis of research. *Journal of Learning Disabilities, 37*(2), 105–118.

Kinsella, K. (2005, October). *Preparing for effective vocabulary instruction*. Aiming High. Accessed at www.scoe.org/docs/ah/AH_kinsella1.pdf on November 6, 2024.

Kinsella, K. (2012, December). Cutting to the Common Core: Communicating on the same wavelength. *Language Magazine, 12*(4), 18–25.

Kintsch, W. (1998). *Comprehension: A paradigm for cognition.* Cambridge University Press.

Kintsch, W., & Kozminsky, E. (1977). Summarizing stories after reading and listening. *Journal of Educational Psychology, 69*(5), 491–499.

Kintsch, W., & van Dijk, T. A. (1978). Toward a model of text comprehension and production. *Psychological Review, 85*(5), 363–394.

Kirchhoff, C., & Mision, M. (2022). Audio-assisted extensive reading: Learners' experience and attitudes. *The Reading Matrix: An International Online Journal, 22*(2), 1–12.

Klein, P. D. (1999). Reopening inquiry into cognitive processes in writing-to-learn. *Educational Psychology Review, 11*(3), 203–270.

Knickerbocker, J. L., & Rycik, J. A. (2006). Reexamining literature study in the middle grades: A critical response framework. *American Secondary Education, 34*(3), 43–56.

Knipper, K. J., & Duggan, T. J. (2006). Writing to learn across the curriculum: Tools for comprehension in content area classes. *The Reading Teacher, 59*(5), 462–470.

Kodan, H., & Akyol, H. (2018). Effects of choral, repeated and assisted reading strategies on reading and reading comprehension skills of poor readers. *Education and Science, 43*(193), 159–179.

Kucan, L., & Beck, I. L. (1997). Thinking aloud and reading comprehension research: Inquiry, instruction, and social interaction. *Review of Educational Research, 67*(3), 271–299.

Lehr, F., Osborn, J., & Hiebert, E. H. (2005). *A focus on comprehension.* Pacific Resources for Education and Learning. Accessed at https://textproject.org/wp-content/uploads/books/Lehr-Osborn-Hiebert-2005-A-Focus-on-Comprehension-booklet.pdf on November 6, 2024.

Leitch, T. (2023). *Decodable readers versus leveled text: A quantitative research methods proposal* [Master's thesis, Minnesota State University Moorhead]. RED: A Repository of Digital Collections. https://red.mnstate.edu/cgi/viewcontent.cgi?article=1903&context=thesis

Lennon, C., & Burdick, H. (2004, April). *The Lexile framework as an approach for reading measurement and success.* MetaMetrics. Accessed at https://metametricsinc.com/wp-content/uploads/2017/07/The-Lexile-Framework-for-Reading.pdf on November 6, 2024.

Levin, J. R., & Pressley, M. (1981). Improving children's prose comprehension: Selected strategies that seem to succeed. In C. M. Santa & B. L. Hayes (Eds.), *Children's prose comprehension: Research and practice* (pp. 44–71). International Reading Association.

Liff Manz, S. (2002). A strategy for previewing textbooks: Teaching readers to become THIEVES. *The Reading Teacher, 55*(5), 434–435.

Lintner, T. (2010). Using children's literature to promote critical geographic awareness in elementary classrooms. *The Social Studies, 101*(1), 17–21.

Lupo, S. M., Berry, A., Thacker, E., Sawyer, A., & Merritt, J. (2020). Rethinking text sets to support knowledge building and interdisciplinary learning. *The Reading Teacher, 73*(4), 513–524.

Lupo, S. M., Strong, J. Z., Lewis, W., Walpole, S., & McKenna, M. C. (2018). Building background knowledge through reading: Rethinking text sets. *Journal of Adolescent and Adult Literacy, 61*(4), 433–444.

Lyon, G. R., & Goldberg, M. (2024, Winter). Structured literacy: Grounded in the science of reading. *Perspectives on Language and Literacy, 50*(1), 19–27.

Mancilla-Martinez, J., & Lesaux, N. K. (2010). Predictors of reading comprehension for struggling readers: The case of Spanish-speaking language minority learners. *Journal of Educational Psychology, 102*(3), 701–711.

Marinaccio, J. (2012). *The most effective pre-reading strategies for comprehension* [Master's thesis, St. John Fisher University]. Fisher Digital Publications. https://fisherpub.sjf.edu/cgi/viewcontent.cgi?referer=&httpsredir=1&article=1209&context=education_ETD_masters

Martohardjono, G., Otheguy, R., Gabriele, A., de Goeas-Malone, M., Szupica-Pyrzanowski, M., Troseth, E., et al. (2005). The role of syntax in reading comprehension: A study of bilingual readers. In J. Cohen, K. T. McAlister, K. Rolstad, & J. MacSwan (Eds.), *Proceedings of the 4th International Symposium on Bilingualism* (pp. 1522–1544). Cascadilla Press.

Marzano, R. J. (2004). *Building background knowledge for academic achievement: Research on what works in schools.* ASCD.

Marzec-Stawiarska, M. (2016). The influence of summary writing on the development of reading skills in a foreign language. *System, 59*, 90–99.

McCarney, R. (2015). *The way to school.* Second Story Press.

McCarthy, K. S., & McNamara, D. S. (2021). The multidimensional knowledge in text comprehension framework. *Educational Psychologist, 56*(3), 196–214.

McElvain, C. M. (2010). Transactional literature circles and the reading comprehension of English learners in the mainstream classroom. *Journal of Research in Reading, 33*(2), 178–205.

Mede, E. (2010). The effects of instruction of graphic organizers in terms of students' attitudes towards reading in English. *Procedia: Social and Behavioral Sciences, 2*(2), 322–325.

Miller, G. E. (1985). The effects of general and specific self-instruction training on children's comprehension monitoring performances during reading. *Reading Research Quarterly, 20*(5), 616–628.

Miranda, J. L. W. (2011). Effect of graphic organizers on the reading comprehension of an English language learner with a learning disability. *Second Language Studies, 30*(1), 95–183.

Mohawk Valley Community College Libraries. (2023, September 5). *What is a Lexile ranking?* Accessed at https://mvcc.libguides.com/kidlit/lexile on January 12, 2025.

Mokhtari, K., & Thompson, H. B. (2006). How problems of reading fluency and comprehension are related to difficulties in syntactic awareness skills among fifth graders. *Reading Research and Instruction, 46*(1), 73–94.

Morgan, A., Wilcox, B. R., & Eldredge, J. L. (2000). Effect of difficulty levels on second-grade delayed readers using dyad reading. *The Journal of Educational Research, 94*(2), 113–119.

Morris, D., Bloodgood, J. W., Lomax, R. G., & Perney, J. (2003). Developmental steps in learning to read: A longitudinal study in kindergarten and first grade. *Reading Research Quarterly, 38*(3), 302–328.

Munson, D. (2000). *Enemy pie* (T. Calahan King, Illus.). Chronicle Books.

Murphy, P. K., Wilkinson, I. A. G., Soter, A. O., Hennessey, M. N., & Alexander, J. F. (2009). Examining the effects of classroom discussion on students' comprehension of text: A meta-analysis. *Journal of Educational Psychology, 101*(3), 740–764.

Murphy, S. J. (1997). *Betcha!* (S. D. Schindler, Illus.). HarperCollins.

National Council for Curriculum and Assessment. (2015, September). *Focus on learning: Learning intentions and success criteria* [Workshop]. Author. Accessed at https://ncca.ie/media/1927/assessment-workshop-1_en.pdf on November 8, 2024.

National Council for the Social Studies. (n.d.). *National curriculum standards for social studies: A framework for teaching, learning, and assessment.* Accessed at www.socialstudies.org/standards/national-curriculum-standards-social-studies on February 14, 2025.

National Governors Association Center for Best Practices & Council of Chief State School Officers. (2010). *Common Core State Standards for English language arts and literacy in history/social studies, science, and technical subjects, Appendix A.* Authors. Accessed at https://docs.google.com/gview?url=https%3A%2F%2Fachievethecore.org%2Fcontent%2Fupload%2Fcorestandards_appendix_a_text_complexity_ela.pdf&embedded=true on November 6, 2024.

National Reading Panel. (2000). *Teaching children to read: An evidence-based assessment of the scientific research literature on reading and its implications for reading instruction: Reports of the subgroups.* Authors. Accessed at www.nichd.nih.gov/sites/default/files/publications/pubs/nrp/Documents/report.pdf on November 6, 2024.

National School Reform Faculty. (2015). *Four A's text protocol.* Accessed at www.nsrfharmony.org/wp-content/uploads/2017/10/FourAsTextProtocol-N.pdf?snoball_referral=4qZE on February 26, 2025.

NGSS Lead States. (2013). *Next Generation Science Standards: For states, by states.* National Academies Press.

No Child Left Behind (NCLB) Act of 2001, Pub. L. No. 107-110, § 115, Stat. 1425 (2002).

Nolte, R. Y., & Singer, H. (1985). Active comprehension: Teaching a process of reading comprehension and its effects on reading achievement. *The Reading Teacher, 39*(1), 24–31.

Norman, R. R. (2010). Picture this: Processes prompted by graphics in informational text. *Literacy Teaching and Learning, 14*(1–2), 1–39.

Numeroff, L. (1985). *If you give a mouse a cookie* (F. Bond, Illus.). Harper & Row.

Numeroff, L. (2008). *If you give a cat a cupcake* (F. Bond, Illus.). Laura Geringer Books.

Oakhill, J. (1993). Children's difficulties in reading comprehension. *Educational Psychology Review, 5*(3), 223–237.

O'Connor, R. E., Swanson, H. L., & Geraghty, C. (2010). Improvement in reading rate under independent and difficult text levels: Influences on word and comprehension skills. *Journal of Educational Psychology, 102*(1), 1–19.

Palmer, B. C., Shackelford, V. S., Miller, S. C., & Leclere, J. T. (2006). Bridging two worlds: Reading comprehension, figurative language instruction, and the English-language learner. *Journal of Adolescent and Adult Literacy, 50*(4), 258–267.

Ponce, H. R., Mayer, R. E., López, M. J., & Loyola, M. S. (2018). Adding interactive graphic organizers to a whole-class slideshow lesson. *Instructional Science, 46*(6), 973–988.

Pondiscio, R. (2014, September 29). Leveled reading: The making of a literacy myth. *Education Next.* Accessed at www.educationnext.org/leveled-reading-making-literacy-myth on November 6, 2024.

Powell, W. R., & Dunkeld, C. G. (1971). Validity of the IRI reading levels. *Elementary English, 48*(6), 637–642.

Pressley, M., & Afflerbach, P. (1995). *Verbal protocols of reading: The nature of constructively responsive reading*. Routledge.

Price, L. H., Bradley, B. A., & Smith, J. M. (2012). A comparison of preschool teachers' talk during storybook and information book read-alouds. *Early Childhood Research Quarterly, 27*(3), 426–440.

Raddi, B. (2018). *The effects of the choral and echo reading strategies on a second grade student with dyslexia* [Master's thesis, Caldwell University]. ProQuest. www.proquest.com/openview/bea2b5bf21b62cb1715bef8061c95c9f/1?pq-origsite=gscholar&cbl=18750

Raphael, T. E. (1986). Teaching question answer relationships, revisited. *The Reading Teacher, 39*(6), 516–522.

Raphael, T. E., & Au, K. H. (2005). QAR: Enhancing comprehension and test taking across grades and content areas. *The Reading Teacher, 59*(3), 206–221.

Raphael, T. E., McMahon, S. I., Goatley, V. J., Bentley, J. L., Boyd, F. B., Pardo, L. S., et al. (1992). Research directions: Literature and discussion in the reading program. *Language Arts, 69*(1), 54–61.

Rathmann, P. (1995). *Officer Buckle and Gloria*. Putnam.

Reading Rockets. (n.d.). *Framed paragraphs*. Accessed at www.readingrockets.org/classroom/classroom-strategies/framed-paragraphs on November 6, 2024.

Ringler, L. H., & Weber, C. K. (1984). *A language-thinking approach to reading: Diagnosis and teaching*. Harcourt Brace Jovanovich.

Robinson, D. H., Katayama, A. D., Beth, A., Odom, S., Hsieh, Y.-P., & Vanderveen, A. (2006). Increasing text comprehension and graphic note taking using a partial graphic organizer. *The Journal of Educational Research, 100*(2), 103–111.

Roehling, J. V., Hebert, M., Nelson, J. R., & Bohaty, J. J. (2017). Text structure strategies for improving expository reading comprehension. *The Reading Teacher, 71*(1), 71–82.

Rosa Le Bron, T. J. (2020). Creating a sentence frame toolkit based on third grade writing standards to support the writing instruction of Spanish-speaking English learners. *Honors Undergraduate Theses*. 754. https://stars.library.ucf.edu/honorstheses/754

Rosenshine, B., Meister, C., & Chapman, S. (1996). Teaching students to generate questions: A review of the intervention studies. *Review of Educational Research, 66*(2), 181–221.

Roskos, K. A., Christie, J. F., & Richgels, D. J. (2003). The essentials of early literacy instruction. *Young Children, 58*(2), 52–60.

Ruurs, M. (2015). *School days around the world* (A. Feagan, Illus.). Kids Can Press.

Saddler, B., Asaro-Saddler, K., Moeyaert, M., & Cuccio-Slichko, J. (2019). Teaching summary writing to students with learning disabilities via strategy instruction. *Reading and Writing Quarterly, 35*(6), 572–586.

Sáenz, L. M., Fuchs, L. S., & Fuchs, D. (2005). Peer-assisted learning strategies for English language learners with learning disabilities. *Exceptional Children, 71*(3), 231–247.

Sajid, M. K. M., & Kassim, H. (2019). The effects of reading aloud strategies on text level difficulties, reading proficiency and reading comprehension skill. *International Journal of Language Education and Applied Linguistics, 9*(1), 85–97.

Samuels, S. J. (1987). Factors that influence listening and reading comprehension. In R. Horowitz & S. J. Samuels (Eds.), *Comprehending oral and written language* (pp. 295–325). Emerald.

Samuels, S. J., & Dahl, P. R. (1975). Establishing appropriate purpose for reading and its effect on flexibility of reading rate. *Journal of Educational Psychology, 67*(1), 38–43.

Scales, R. Q., & Tracy, K. N. (2017). Using text sets to facilitate critical thinking in sixth graders. *Literacy Research and Instruction, 56*(2), 132–157.

Scott, C. M. (2009). A case for the sentence in reading comprehension. *Language, Speech, and Hearing Services in Schools, 40*(2), 184–191.

Sedita, J. (2013). Learning to write and writing to learn. In M. C. Hougen (Ed.), *Fundamentals of literacy instruction and assessment, 6–12* (pp. 97–114). Brookes.

Sedita, J. (2020, June 2). *Syntactic awareness: Teaching sentence structure (part 1)* [Blog post]. Accessed at https://keystoliteracy.com/blog/syntactic-awareness-teaching-sentence-structure-part-1 on November 6, 2024.

Selsam, M. E. (1995). *Big tracks, little tracks: Following animal prints* (M. H. Donnelly, Illus.). HarperCollins.

Sendak, M. (1963). *Where the wild things are* (M. Sendak, Illus.). Harper & Row.

Shanahan, T. (1983). The informal reading inventory and the instructional level: The study that never took place. In L. M. Gentile, M. L. Kamil, & J. S. Blanchard (Eds.), *Reading research revisited* (pp. 577–580). Merrill.

Shanahan, T. (2011, August 21). *Rejecting instructional level theory* [Blog post]. Accessed at www.shanahanonliteracy.com/blog/rejecting-instructional-level-theory on November 6, 2024.

Shanahan, T. (2014). Should we teach students at their reading levels? Consider the research when personalizing your lesson plans. *Reading Today, 32*(2), 14–15.

Shanahan, T. (2020). Limiting children to books they can already read: Why it reduces their opportunity to learn. *American Educator, 44*(2), 13–17.

Shanahan, T. (2024, June 1). *Should we teach with decodable text?* [Blog post]. Accessed at www.shanahanonliteracy.com/blog/should-we-teach-with-decodable-text-1 on November 6, 2024.

Shanahan, T., Fisher, D., & Frey, N. (2016). The challenge of challenging text. In M. Scherer (Ed.), *On developing readers: Readings from* Educational Leadership (pp. 100–109). ASCD.

Shanahan, T., & Shanahan, C. (2012). What is disciplinary literacy and why does it matter? *Topics in Language Disorders, 32*(1), 7–18.

Shapiro, A. M. (2004). How including prior knowledge as a subject variable may change outcomes of learning research. *American Educational Research Journal, 41*(1), 159–189.

Shimada, M.-M. M. (2017). *Third grade science teachers' perspectives on implementing sentence frames and word banks during science lectures to increase the writing levels of English language learners* [Honors undergraduate thesis, University of Central Florida]. STARS. https://stars.library.ucf.edu/cgi/viewcontent.cgi?article=1221&context=honorstheses

Short, K. G. (1993). Making connections across literature and life. In K. E. Holland, R. A. Hungerford, & S. B. Ernst (Eds.), *Journeying: Children responding to literature* (pp. 284–301). Heinemann.

Sindelar, P. T., Monda, L. E., & O'Shea, L. J. (1990). Effects of repeated readings on instructional- and mastery-level readers. *The Journal of Educational Research, 83*(4), 220–226.

Smith, A. P., & Jones, D. M. (Eds.). (1992). *Handbook of human performance: Vol. 2. Health and performance*. Academic Press.

Smith, R., Snow, P., Serry, T., & Hammond, L. (2021). The role of background knowledge in reading comprehension: A critical review. *Reading Psychology, 42*(3), 214–240.

Stahl, S. A., & Fairbanks, M. M. (1986). The effects of vocabulary instruction: A model-based meta-analysis. *Review of Educational Research, 56*(1), 72–110.

Stange, T. V. (2013). Exploring text level difficulty and matching texts for reading achievement. *Education Matters, 1*(2), 111–128.

Stanovich, K. E. (1986). Matthew effects in reading: Some consequences of individual differences in the acquisition of literacy. *Reading Research Quarterly, 21*(4), 360–407.

Sticht, T. G., Beck, L. J., Hauke, R. N., Kleiman, G. M., & James, J. H. (1974). *Auding and reading: A developmental model.* Human Resources Research Organization. Accessed at https://citeseerx.ist.psu.edu/document?repid=rep1&type=pdf&doi=fe1e93d30aac13bf16a4ad2eb786734494f3f12c on November 6, 2024.

Swain, K. D., Leader-Janssen, E. M., & Conley, P. (2013). Effects of repeated reading and listening passage preview on oral reading fluency. *Reading Improvement, 50*(1), 12–18.

Taboada, A., & Guthrie, J. T. (2006). Contributions of student questioning and prior knowledge to construction of knowledge from reading information text. *Journal of Literacy Research, 38*(1), 1–35.

Taylor, N. E., Wade, M. R., & Yekovich, F. R. (1985). The effects of text manipulation and multiple reading strategies on the reading performance of good and poor readers. *Reading Research Quarterly, 20*(5), 566–574.

Therrien, W. J. (2004). Fluency and comprehension gains as a result of repeated reading: A meta-analysis. *Remedial and Special Education, 25*(4), 252–261.

Thompson, C. K., & Shapiro, L. P. (2007). Complexity in treatment of syntactic deficits. *American Journal of Speech Language Pathology, 16*(1), 30–42.

Titsworth, S., Mazer, J. P., Goodboy, A. K., Bolkan, S., & Myers, S. A. (2015). Two meta-analyses exploring the relationship between teacher clarity and student learning. *Communication Education, 64*(4), 385–418.

Treiman, R. (2018). What research tells us about reading instruction. *Psychological Science in the Public Interest, 19*(1), 1–4.

Trottier Brown, L., Mohr, K. A. J., Wilcox, B. R., & Barrett, T. S. (2018). The effects of dyad reading and text difficulty on third-graders' reading achievement. *The Journal of Educational Research, 111*(5), 541–553. https://dx.doi.org/10.1080/00220671.2017.1310711

Turpie, J. J., & Paratore, J. R. (1995). Using repeated reading to promote reading success in a heterogeneously grouped first grade. In K. A. Hinchman, D. J. Leu, & C. K. Kinzer (Eds.), *Perspectives on literacy research and practice: Forty-fourth yearbook of the National Reading Conference* (pp. 255–264). National Reading Conference.

Tyner, A., & Kabourek, S. (2021). How social studies improves elementary literacy. *Social Education, 85*(1), 32–39.

Valencia Goodall, M., Gomez, M., & Webster, D. W. (2024). Effective instruction: The intersection of structured literacy and second-language acquisition for multilingual learners. *The Reading League Journal.* Accessed at www.thereadingleague.org/wp-content/uploads/2024/06/the-reading-league-journal-may-2024-effective-instruction.pdf on February 27, 2025.

Viorst, J. (1972). *Alexander and the terrible, horrible, no good, very bad day* (R. Cruz, Illus.). Atheneum.

Vygotsky, L. S. (1978). *Mind in society: The development of higher psychological processes*. Harvard University Press.

Webb, N. L. (2002, March 28). *Depth-of-knowledge levels for four content areas*. Accessed at https://dpi.wi.gov/sites/default/files/imce/assessment/pdf/All%20content%20areas%20%20DOK%20levels.pdf on February 27, 2025.

Wexler, N. (2019). *The knowledge gap: The hidden cause of America's broken education system—and how to fix it*. Avery.

Wexler, N. (2021, September 8). New data shows building knowledge can boost reading comprehension. *Forbes*. Accessed at www.forbes.com/sites/nataliewexler/2021/09/08/new-data-shows-building-knowledge-can-boost-reading-comprehension on November 6, 2024.

Wilkinson, I. A. G., Murphy, P. K., & Binici, S. (2015). Dialogue-intensive pedagogies for promoting reading comprehension: What we know, what we need to know. In L. B. Resnick, C. S. C. Asterhan, & S. N. Clarke (Eds.), *Socializing intelligence through academic talk and dialogue* (pp. 37–50). American Educational Research Association.

Wilkinson, I. A. G., & Nelson, K. (2013). Role of discussion in reading comprehension. In J. Hattie & E. M. Anderman (Eds.), *International guide to student achievement* (pp. 299–302). Routledge.

Williams, J. P. (2005). Instruction in reading comprehension for primary-grade students: A focus on text structure. *The Journal of Special Education, 39*(1), 6–18.

Willingham, D. (2006). How knowledge helps. *American Educator, 30*(1), 30–37.

Willingham, D. (2012, March 7). *School time, knowledge, and reading comprehension* [Blog post]. Accessed at www.danielwillingham.com/daniel-willingham-science-and-education-blog/school-time-knowledge-and-reading-comprehension on November 6, 2024.

Wittrock, M. C. (1992). Knowledge acquisition and comprehension. In M. C. Alkin (Ed.), *Encyclopedia of educational research* (6th ed., pp. 699–705). Macmillan.

Wolf, M. K., Crosson, A. C., & Resnick, L. B. (2005). Classroom talk for rigorous reading comprehension instruction. *Reading Psychology, 26*(1), 27–53.

Zheng, Y. (2012). Exploring long-term productive vocabulary development in an EFL context: The role of motivation. *System, 40*(1), 104–119.

Zulianti, H., & Hastomo, T. (2022). Partner reading strategy: An effective strategy for improving students' reading comprehension. *Premise: Journal of English Education and Applied Linguistics, 11*(1), 175–189.

Zwiers, J. (2004). *Developing academic thinking skills in grades 6–12: A handbook of multiple intelligence activities*. International Reading Association.

INDEX

A

academic discussions. *See* engaging in structured academic discussion
activating prior knowledge. *See also* prior knowledge
    before-reading scaffolding strategy, 21, 25–29
    building background knowledge and, 30
    list of strategies, 17, 20
active reading. *See* engaging all students in active reading
advanced understanding strategies, 109. *See also* after-reading scaffolding strategies
after-reading scaffolding strategies. *See also* scaffolding
    about, 109–110
    analyzing sentence structure using syntactic awareness, 136–140
    discussing with sentence frames and word banks, 132–136
    engaging in extended writing tasks, 118–121
    graphic organizer planning, 88, 89
    list of strategies, 17, 108
    providing sentence and paragraph frames, 121–125
    scaffolding with partially completed graphic organizers, 114–118
    summarizing, 125–132
    using text-dependent questions for collaborative discussion, 110–114
alphabetic principle, 10, 142
analyzing sentence structure using syntactic awareness. *See also* syntactic awareness
    after-reading scaffolding strategy, 110, 136–140
    list of strategies, 17, 108
anchor charts, 40, 41, 112, 127
anticipation-reaction guides, 26, 27. *See also* activating prior knowledge
Asaro-Saddler, K., 126
asking and answering questions. *See also* questions
    during-reading scaffolding strategy, 68, 80–84
    list of strategies, 17, 66
audio-assisted reading question planner, 49. *See also* questions; reading text with audio assistance

B

Babbitt, N., 137–138
background knowledge. *See* building background knowledge
before-reading scaffolding strategies. *See also* scaffolding
    about, 21–24
    activating prior knowledge, 25–29
    building background knowledge, 29–32
    discussing text structure, 53–59
    establishing a purpose for reading, 22–25
    front-loading vocabulary, 32–38
    graphic organizer planning, 88, 89
    list of strategies, 17, 20
    making predictions, 43–46
    previewing the text, 39–43
    reading aloud to students, 50–53
    reading text with audio assistance, 47–50
    using text sets to build knowledge, 59–64
Bett's levels of text difficulty, 6–8
Bray Donnelly, W., 133
Brown, P., 29
building background knowledge
    before-reading scaffolding strategy, 21, 29–32
    list of strategies, 17, 20
    planning tool for, 32
    using text sets to build knowledge and, 60
building the case for challenging text. *See* challenging texts

C

cause and effect graphic organizer, 57. *See also* graphic organizers

challenging texts
- about, 5–6
- debunking the instructional text theory and, 6–8
- defining, 8–9
- ensuring grade-level difficulty and, 14–15
- finding appropriately challenging texts, 148
- understanding how to use the twenty-five scaffolding strategies, 16–19
- using for developing readers (grades 2 and up), 13–14
- using for early readers (grades K-1), 10–13

choral reading
- active reading and, 68, 69, 70, 73, 150
- decodable text routines and, 12
- dyad reading and, 147

chunking text
- chunking planner, 93
- during-reading scaffolding strategy, 67, 90–91
- excerpt from *Enemy Pie* with chunking suggestions, 92
- list of strategies, 17, 66

cloze reading, 68, 69, 70, 73, 150

collaborative discussions. *See* using text-dependent questions for collaborative discussion

comparing and contrasting
- building background knowledge and, 31
- compare and contrast graphic organizer, 56. *See also* graphic organizers

concept maps, 86, 146

concepts and skills, front-loading key vocabulary, 146–147

connected texts, 9, 10–13, 16

connections. *See* making connections

core ELA programs
- multilanguage learners and, 34
- using your ELA core program effectively, 142–143

Cuccio-Slichko, J., 126

D

decodable texts, 9, 10, 11–12, 13

Depth of Knowledge (DOK) model, 81–82, 84

description
- description graphic organizer, 56. *See also* graphic organizers
- discussing text structure and, 57

discussing text structure
- before-reading scaffolding strategy, 22, 53–59
- graphic organizers by text structure, 55–57
- list of strategies, 17, 20
- text structure planning template, 59

discussing with sentence frames and word banks. *See also* sentence frames
- after-reading scaffolding strategy, 110, 132–136
- instructional design and delivery for using sentence frames or word banks, 135
- instructional planning template for sentence frames and word banks, 135
- list of strategies, 17, 108

discussions
- academic discussions. *See* engaging in structured academic discussion
- collaborative discussions. *See* using text-dependent questions for collaborative discussion

duet reading
- active reading and, 68, 69, 71, 73, 150
- decodable text routines and, 12

Duggan, T., 98

during-reading scaffolding strategies. *See also* scaffolding
- about, 67–68
- asking and answering questions, 80–84
- chunking text, 90–93
- engaging all students in active reading, 68–75
- engaging in structured academic discussion, 94–97
- list of strategies, 17, 66
- making connections, 76–80
- summarizing texts using paragraph shrinking, 102–107
- using graphic organizers, 84–90
- writing to learn, 97–101

dyad reading, 8–9, 147–149

E

echo reading, 68, 69, 70, 73, 150

engaging all students in active reading
- active reading engagement techniques poster, 73
- active reading engagement techniques strategy planner, 75
- during-reading scaffolding strategy, 67, 68–75
- list of strategies, 17, 66

engaging in extended writing tasks
- after-reading scaffolding strategy, 110, 118–121
- list of strategies, 17, 108

engaging in structured academic discussion
- during-reading scaffolding strategy, 68, 94–97
- list of strategies, 17, 66

establishing a purpose for reading
- before-reading scaffolding strategy, 22–25
- list of strategies, 17, 20
- making predictions and, 43

explicit instruction
   delivering explicit instruction effectively, 144–145
   explicit vocabulary instruction, 35–38, 146
expository texts, 54, 55

F

finger tracking, 69, 149
fishbone graphic organizers, 86. *See also* graphic organizers
fluency interventions, 7
Four A's, 113
Frayer models, 86
front-loading vocabulary. *See also* vocabulary
   before-reading scaffolding strategy, 21, 32–38
   discussing with sentence frames and word banks and, 134
   list of strategies, 17, 20
   small-group and partner instruction and, 146–147
frustration reading level, 6–8, 9

G

grade-level text difficulty, 14–15
graffiti walls, 113–114
graphic organizers. *See also* scaffolding with partially completed graphic organizers; using graphic organizers
   activating prior knowledge and, 26
   common graphic organizers and their primary uses, 86–87
   graphic organizer planning and implementation tool, 88
   graphic organizer planning template, 89
   graphic organizers by text structure, 55–57

H

hand signals, 95. *See also* talk moves

I

I Do, We Do, You Do model, 144
idioms, 30
incorporating scaffolding strategies into instruction. *See also* scaffolding
   about, 141
   small-group and partner instruction, 145–151
   whole-group instruction, 141–145
independent reading level, 6–8, 9
informational texts, 13, 44
Institute of Education Sciences, 13
instructional planning sequence for "The Three Little Pigs," 116–117
instructional reading level, 6–8, 9
instructional texts, debunking the instructional text theory, 6–8
interaction with the text strategies, 67. *See also* during-reading scaffolding strategies
introduction
   what's in this book, 3–4
   why I wrote this book, 2–3

J

"just right" texts, 5

K

key questions/question words, use of, 98–99
Klein, P., 118–119
Knipper, K., 98
knowledge demands, 18
K-W-L charts, 26, 27

L

language conventionality and clarity, 18
learning intentions, 23
learning logs, T-chart, 100
levels of meaning or purpose, 18
levels of text difficulty, 6–8
Lexile level, 14–15, 148
limited knowledge strategies, 21–22
listen, pause, sketch activities, 51
listening, four L's of productive listening, 111–112
literacy
   building knowledge in the content areas, 145
   reading development, aspects critical to, 142
literary texts, 13, 43, 44
lived experience and relationships, 77

M

Make It Stick: The Science of Successful Learning (Brown, Roediger, and McDaniel), 29
making connections
   during-reading scaffolding strategy, 67, 76–80
   list of strategies, 17, 66
   making predictions and, 43
"Making Connections Across Literature and Life" (Short), 76
making predictions
   before-reading scaffolding strategy, 21, 43–46
   list of strategies, 17, 20
   prediction chart example, 46
matching students to text, 6–7

McDaniel, M., 29
mentor texts, 57, 119, 120
misconception checks, 100
mnemonics, 40, 41, 42, 127
Moeyaert, M., 126
multilanguage learners (MLLs)
    asking and answering questions and, 80
    chunking text and, 90
    content comprehension and, 23
    core ELA programs and, 34
    discussing with sentence frames and word banks, 134
    duet reading and, 73
    engaging in structured academic discussion and, 96
    extended writing tasks and, 119
    graphic organizers and, 84, 115
    idioms and, 30
    instructional routines and, 127
    lived experience and relationships and, 77
    mnemonics and, 42
    reading aloud to students and, 51
    reading text with audio assistance and, 49
    sentence and paragraph frames and, 122
    signal words and, 54
    summarizing texts using paragraph shrinking and, 103
    syntactic awareness and, 136
    text sets and, 61
    visuals and, 27, 45
    writing to learn and, 100
multimedia
    building background knowledge and, 31
    front-loading key vocabulary, concepts, and skills, 146
    text sets and, 61
my question, my final answer example, 83

N

narrative texts, 54, 126

O

open-ended questions, 94–95, 97, 110, 111. *See also* questions
oral language strategies, 68, 110. *See also* after-reading scaffolding strategies; during-reading scaffolding strategies
organization of the text strategies, 22. *See also* before-reading scaffolding strategies

P

paragraph shrinking. *See* summarizing texts using paragraph shrinking
partners. *See also* small-group and partner instruction
    partner reading, 68, 69, 71, 73, 150
    strategic partnering, 74–75
    summarizing texts using paragraph shrinking and, 102–103
phonemic awareness, 11, 142
phonics
    decodable text routine as part of an explicit phonics lesson, 12
    defining challenging texts and, 9
    key components of an explicit phonics lesson, 11
picture books, 31, 44
picture/image cards, 50–51, 52
popcorn reading, 68
predictions. *See* making predictions
previewing the text
    before-reading scaffolding strategy, 22, 39–43
    decodable text routines and, 12
    list of strategies, 17, 20
prior knowledge. *See also* activating prior knowledge
    background knowledge and, 29
    prior knowledge strategies, 21
problem and solution graphic organizer, 56. *See also* graphic organizers
providing sentence and paragraph frames
    after-reading scaffolding strategy, 110, 121–125
    list of strategies, 17, 108

Q

QAR (question answer relationships) approach, 76–79
qualitative text features, 15, 18
quantitative text features, 15, 18
questions. *See also* asking and answering questions; using text-dependent questions for collaborative discussion
    audio-assisted reading question planner, 49
    DOK question planner, 84
    key questions/question words, use of, 98–99
    my question, my final answer example, 83
    open-ended questions, 94–95, 97, 110, 111
    QAR (question answer relationships) approach, 76–79
    question and answer graphic organizer, 57
    question and evidence two-column chart, 99
    question generation, 80–82
    questions to build syntactic awareness, 137
    sample questions for monitoring and understanding, 48

R

reading, establishing a purpose for. *See* establishing a purpose for reading

reading aloud to students
    before-reading scaffolding strategy, 22, 50–53
    list of strategies, 17, 20
reading text with audio assistance
    audio-assisted reading question planner, 49
    before-reading scaffolding strategy, 22, 47–50
    list of strategies, 17, 20
repeated reading, 149–151
Roe, C., 133
Roediger, H., 29
round robin reading, 68

S

Saddler, B., 126
sample questions for monitoring and understanding, 48. *See also* questions
Save the Last Word for ME, 112–113
scaffolding. *See also specific scaffolding strategies*
    dyad reading and, 147–149
    frustration reading level and, 8
    incorporating scaffolding strategies into instruction, 141–151
    list of strategies, 17
    scaffolding strategies to use after reading. *See* after-reading scaffolding strategies
    scaffolding strategies to use before reading. *See* before-reading scaffolding strategies
    scaffolding strategies to use during reading. *See* during-reading scaffolding strategies
    understanding how to use the twenty-five scaffolding strategies, 16–19
scaffolding with partially completed graphic organizers. *See also* graphic organizers
    after-reading scaffolding strategy, 109, 114–118
    list of strategies, 17, 108
sentence frames. *See also* discussing with sentence frames and word banks; providing sentence and paragraph frames
    collaborative discussion sentence frames, 112
    engaging in extended writing tasks and, 96
    instructional design and delivery for using sentence frames or word banks, 135
    instructional planning template for sentence frames and word banks, 135
    MLLs and academic language and, 96
sequence graphic organizer, 55. *See also* graphic organizers
Short, K., 76
signal words, 54, 55, 59
simple texts, 31, 32, 147
skills, front-loading key vocabulary, concepts and, 146–147

small-group and partner instruction
    about, 145–146
    dyad reading, scaffolding with, 147–149
    front-loading key vocabulary, concepts, and skills, 146–147
    repeated reading and, 149–151
Somebody Wanted But So Then (routine), 128, 131
sound-spelling patterns, 10, 11
speech bubble cards, 50–51, 52
story maps, 55, 86
strategic partnering, 74–75
structure, qualitative domains of complex texts, 18
student anthologies, 10, 12, 13, 50, 102
success criteria, 23
summarizing
    after-reading scaffolding strategy, 110, 125–132
    list of strategies, 17, 108
    Somebody Wanted But So Then (routine), 128, 131
    WINDOW summary method, 127–130, 132
summarizing texts using paragraph shrinking
    during-reading scaffolding strategy, 68, 102–107
    list of strategies, 17, 66
    paragraph shrinking instructional routine, 104–105
    paragraph shrinking prompt cards, 106
syntactic awareness, 136, 137. *See also* analyzing sentence structure using syntactic awareness

T

talk moves, 94, 95, 97
Tatum, A., 7
T-chart learning log, 100
text sets, 59, 61, 64. *See also* using text sets to build knowledge
text structure planning template, 59. *See also* discussing text structure
THIEVES instructional routine, 40, 41, 42. *See also* previewing the text
timeline graphic organizers, 86. *See also* graphic organizers
Tuck Everlasting (Babbitt), 137–138

U

using graphic organizers. *See also* graphic organizers
    common graphic organizers and their primary uses, 86–87
    during-reading scaffolding strategy, 68, 84–90
    graphic organizer planning and implementation tool, 88
    graphic organizer planning template, 89
    list of strategies, 17, 66
using text sets to build knowledge

before-reading scaffolding strategy, 22, 59–64
list of strategies, 17, 20
using text-dependent questions for collaborative discussion. *See also* questions
after-reading scaffolding strategy, 109, 110–114
list of strategies, 17, 108

V

Venn diagrams, 56, 86, 117
visuals
activating prior knowledge and, 26
front-loading key vocabulary, concepts, and skills, 146
informational and literary texts and, 44
making predictions and, 45
vocabulary. *See also* front-loading vocabulary
explicit vocabulary instruction, 35–38, 146
teacher tip, 23
tiers of vocabulary words, 33
using text sets to build knowledge and, 60
vocabulary cards, 50–51, 52

W

Wexler, N., 14
whisper reading, 12, 68, 69, 72, 73, 150

whole-group instruction
about, 141
building knowledge in the content areas and, 145
delivering explicit instruction effectively and, 144–145
ELA core program, use of, 142–143
WINDOW summary method, 127–130, 132
word banks. *See also* discussing with sentence frames and word banks
about, 132
instructional design and delivery for using sentence frames or word banks, 135
instructional planning template for sentence frames and word banks, 135
word webs, 56
writing tasks, engaging in extended. *See* engaging in extended writing tasks
writing to learn
during-reading scaffolding strategy, 68, 97–101
list of strategies, 17, 66
written task strategies, 68, 109–110. *See also* after-reading scaffolding strategies; during-reading scaffolding strategies

Z

zone of proximal development (ZPD), 8

Small Groups for Big Readers
Taylar B. Wenzel, Analexis Kennedy, Dena D. Slanda, and Melissa R. Carli
The authors advocate for small-group reading instruction as an effective way for teachers to help all students grow as skilled, developing readers. Through small-group instruction, grades K–5 teachers can better identify individual student learning interests, needs, and goals.
BKG189

Solving the Literacy Puzzle
Norene A. Bunt
Using graphic organizers, assessments, and reflection questions, educators can unpack five core components of literacy instruction within the science of reading framework. This comprehensive guide prepares teachers to confidently implement effective literacy instruction in their classrooms.
BKG158

Read Alouds for All Learners
Molly Ness
In *Read Alouds for All Learners: A Comprehensive Plan for Every Subject, Every Day, Grades PreK–8*, Molly Ness provides a compelling case for the integration, or reintegration, of the read aloud in schools and a step-by-step resource for grades preK–8 educators in classrooms.
BKG116

The Power of Effective Reading Instruction
Karen Gazith
Through research-supported tools and strategies, this book explores how children learn to read and how neuroscience should inform reading practices in schools. Grades K–12 educators will find resources and reproducible tools to effectively implement reading instruction and interventions, no matter the subject taught.
BKG104

Solution Tree | Press

Visit SolutionTree.com or call 800.733.6786 to order.

We don't just help schools make a change, we help them *be* the change

REAL IMPACT. RELEVANT SOLUTIONS. RESULTS-DRIVEN APPROACH.

From funding to faculty retention, the evolving demands schools face can be overwhelming. That's where we come in. With professional development rooted in decades of research and delivered by many of the educators who literally wrote the book on it, we empower schools to achieve meaningful change with real, sustainable results.

The change starts here. We can make it happen together.

See how we can get real results for your school or district.

Scan the code or visit:

SolutionTree.com/Results-Driven

 Solution Tree

LET'S SEE WHAT **WE CAN** DO TOGETHE